PART ONE
GOING UP

1

Somehow, I was born to trade.

A light post and a telegraph pole stand four meters apart against the towering, concave wall of a recycling center at the end of my street, making the perfect impromptu goalposts.

Taking ten giant steps backward and staring upward and between the two posts into the distant distance will reveal the tallest Canary Wharf skyscraper's light winking at you over that high wall.

I spent many evenings playing battered foam footballs around the goalposts in my brother's school uniform and battered school shoes. I watched that tower wink at me when my mom called me home for dinner. A new life seemed to be implied.

I shared more than East London's streets with capitalism's glittering temples. There was also a shared belief. A financial matter. Something about want.

I was always aware of how little money we had and how important it was. I remember my parents giving me a pound coin and sending me to Esso to purchase lemonade as a child. I dropped that pound coin throughout the trip and lost it. I remember crawling under cars and scrabbling in sewers for hours to get that pound coin before returning home empty-handed and crying. It probably took 30 minutes. One pound was a lot of money, and thirty minutes is a long time for a child. I'm not sure I lost my passion for money. But now that I think about it, love may not be the perfect term. Perhaps it was more of a terror, especially as a child. Whatever it was—fear, love, or hunger—became stronger as I grew, and I was continually pursuing those pounds I didn't have. I started selling penny candies in school at 12 and delivering papers 364 days a year for £13 a week at 13. My high school sales career was more adventurous, profitable, and illegal by sixteen. But those tiny kills were never the end game, and every night, as the sun went down, I would look up at those skyscrapers winking at me from the street.

There were many other ways I was not born to trade, yet they are nevertheless significant.

In East London's skyscrapers' shadows, numerous young, hungry, ambitious youths kick shattered footballs around lamp poles and automobiles. Most of them are brilliant, committed, and would sacrifice a lot to put on a tie and cufflinks and go into those tall, glossy money towers. You won't hear Millwall and Bow, Stepney and Mile End, Shadwell and Poplar's proud accents on those trading floors in those glittering skyscrapers where young men earn millions of pounds every year in the heart of what was once East London's docklands. Since I worked on a trading floor, I know. Someone asked me my accent's origin. Just graduated from Oxford.

The 42-story Citibank Tower at Canary Wharf. I entered that building in 2006, when it was the UK's equal second-tallest. In 2007, I went to the top level to observe the view and see my home.

Only conferences and events were held on the Citibank Center's upper floor. This left the entire space unoccupied while not in use. A large blue carpet country with thick glass windows on all sides. I glided across the silent carpet to the window, but I couldn't see my house. East London is invisible from the Citibank Center's 42nd level. Only the 42nd storey of HSBC Tower is visible. The ambitious East London kids love the skyscrapers that cast shadows on their dwellings, but the skyscrapers don't glance back. They regard each other.

Of all the youngsters playing football and peddling sweets in those shadows, I obtained a job on the Citibank trading floor. I'll tell you how I became Citibank's most lucrative trader in the world and why I quit.

The world economy began to decline in these years. Sometimes my sanity faded. Sometimes it does. I didn't treat everyone well. Harry,

GARY STEVENSON

BIOGRAPHY

The Trader Who Saw It All

TABLE OF CONTENTS

Wizard, JB, myself. All the others who deserved names. Please forgive me for sharing your stories. All part of my story, right?

When we were intoxicated adolescents and he was a drunken old man, Anish's granddad would mutter incessantly the only English line he knew.

"Life is life. Game is game."

2

The London School of Economics was my gateway to trading.

LSE isn't a typical university. The university buildings hide in a West End alley as a cluster of offices because they have no great, green campus.

Despite these benign conditions, the global wealthy enthusiastically enroll their children in university. No Russian oligarch, Pakistani Air Force Commander, or Chinese Politburo member seemed to have missed the chance to send an ambitious son, daughter, nephew, or niece to this unremarkable corner of central London to study simultaneous equations for a few years before returning home to take over the mother country, perhaps with a few years at Goldman Sachs or Deloitte.

When I arrived at LSE in 2005 to study maths and economics, I was unusual. Three years ago, I was expelled from high school for selling £3 of cannabis. I tried to form a grime music collective and had a hoodie manufactured with "MC Gaz" on the front and "Cadaverous Crew" in big, stylized lettering on the back. I wore an Ecko tracksuit with a blue and white sweatshirt and running pants to my first lecture. A large navy blue rhino adorned the white hoodie. Before arriving, I knew little about college. However, a schoolmate assured me that an LSE degree would guarantee a high-paying City career, which was enough for me.

Naturally, I didn't fit. Oligarchs in Russia avoided halal fried chicken restaurants. Singaporeans didn't get my accent. I lived with my parents in Ilford, ten miles east of college, to save money. I had just met my first girlfriend, also from Ilford, and spent most of my first year drinking with her on park benches, sneaking her out of my bedroom window and over the railway tracks when my mum came home from work, and only going to university for lectures and classes.

I still wanted to succeed at LSE. No family links or City knowledge. I was short, ugly, and lacked a suit and networking abilities. A lackluster career as a fast-rapping grime MC and two years fluffing pillows at DFS couch store in Beckton were my most remarkable extracurriculars. Since maths had always come effortlessly to me, I saw only one way to get into the City: beat all the Arab millionaires and Chinese industrialists to a top first-class degree and pray to God Goldman Sachs noticed.

The strategy was simple: sit at the front of every lecture and class and make sure I understood everything the professor and teacher said.

The plan worked, and I had a good first year. My honest assessment is that it was simple. I left for the summer thinking my strategy would succeed.

However, my second year at the LSE brought some major changes.

Suddenly, unexpectedly, and seemingly unrelated, practically every student in the year group became a serious junior banker. To my surprise, everyone started acting as if they had employment at Canary Wharf or the City's gleaming towers. People started attending Finance Society Wednesday and Friday gatherings and Investment Society Monday networking events. Their phrases were mostly three-letter acronyms—ABS, IBD, CDS, CDO, M&A—and they discussed "Sales and Trading" and "Securitization." For unknown reasons, many people started wearing business suits to lectures. Rumors spread that tall, broad-chested, well-coiffed, suit-wearing students of nationally-ambiguous-clearly-wealthy provenance had gotten internships at Goldman Sachs, Deutsche Bank, JPMorgan, or Lehman Brothers. Some found full-time jobs.

All students applied for internships. Fifteen, twenty, or more internships. Theoretical interview questions allegedly given to a fictional Statistics or International Relations student spread among students. It became common knowledge that interviewees were asked how many bald Virginians there were. One pupil apparently had five seconds to answer 49 times 49. All students carefully documented 2,401. Inexplicably large lines formed in random campus places. Most queueing students weren't sure what the queue was for when asked. Maybe someone gets an internship at the end. There may be networking opportunities. Twenty or so calculator-wielding students gathered around library computers, spitting out numbers and letters to take Morgan Stanley's online numerical examinations.

I didn't know how to react to my classmates' entire shift in attitude, approach, and priorities. Many stopped attending lectures to focus on networking, job applications, and finance lingo and acronyms. My previously successful method of attending lectures and classes and knowing the content felt horribly insufficient and naïve.

In my first year of university, I made a few wonderful friends, including Matic, a tall, gorgeous, British-raised Slovenian boy who studied arithmetic with me. Matic had sharpened his dress, but not to the extent of many other students. He joined finance societies. He acronymized. He applied. He interviewed. Events he attended.

I questioned Matic how the summer could have changed the student community so drastically.

Gary, what do you mean? Do you know? Second year is internship!"

It works like this. I'll tell you what Matic told me then.

Every LSE student wants a Goldman Sachs job. OR Deutsche Bank. OR Morgan Stanley. Or JPM. Or UBS.

Everyone at LSE and Imperial. Everyone at Warwick. All at Nottingham, Durham, and Bath. Manchester and Birmingham residents want to work there, but they can't unless they know someone in the industry. The Oxford and Cambridge students who aren't fortunate enough to never work want to work there.

Not enough jobs for everyone. Far too little. Additionally, not all jobs are equal. Best job: "Sales and Trading." That employment provides the best hours (12 hours a day, plus weekends off) and pays the most quickly if you're good. Unless you obtain Sales and Trading, you must spend 100-hour weeks in IBD, M&A, or something till your soul dies and then longer. Not making that means working in "Consulting."

Consulting was completely unknown to me. As Matic stated, it may have been toilet cleaning.

Without contacts, you can't find a job without an internship, and the only opportunity to get one is now. Without an internship after second year, you'll need one after third. If you interned after third year, you'd be unemployed for a year because 50% of interns acquire full-time jobs a year later. No investment bank will hire an intern after their third year because they will know they were rejected in the second year and will not want a rejected intern. That concludes. Make or break. Do or die. Decision time for your future. Stop thinking about "Maths and Economics." You must understand CDS. What's M&A? What's IBD? Can you not know Gary? Everyone knows! Send applications. These internships are overapplied, and you have no connections. One can only be obtained by applying to thirty banks. How many have you applied to? None!?!"

There was no answer. I was lost.

Could do math. Could do economics. However, I had nothing in this acronym world. I trusted my teachers back at school: study hard and do well in your exams and you'll get a nice job. I was stupid. I was an idiot.

Matic, though intense, was kind and took pity on me. He took me to a finance society event called "How to Get a Job at an Investment Bank."

In one of LSE's grander, older, brighter lecture theaters, the event was warmly attended. A former investment banker who looked like he was on break from being an extra in a Wall Street movie gave a talk. Pinstriped, slicked-back hair, and tall.

The talk seemed like a stream-of-consciousness monologue on hard work, with each sentence punctuated by words and acronyms I was sure I had heard somewhere but didn't understand, as if it were being delivered in a language I had half-studied in high school but never fully learned. The speaker spoke with incredible energy and walked quickly across the stage. The takeaway was simple: study everything, understand these terminologies, network everyone, apply everywhere, work always, don't sleep. That may not have been the message. I was depressed after the discussion.

I stopped applying for internships, much to Matic's and my regret. I couldn't. Acronyms have never stuck with me. It burdened me too much. The application process began with a CV and cover letter. The others had prepared since they were four. They all appeared to have walked the Sahara, led the Junior UN, played the oboe at the Royal Albert Hall, or something. My CV included six years delivering newspapers, one year as a failed grime rapper, and two years fluffing pillows at a Beckton sofa shop near to a sewage works. The point?

The second unexpected and inexplicable change in my undergraduate experience saved me. People recognized me when I returned to university for my second year. People I had never met before, even suit-wearers, would approach me in the library and start conversing. A Chinese student stopped me in a corridor, looked me up and down fiercely, wordlessly, for ten seconds, then left. Another time, a tall European girl with an unclear accent and great hair wanted to study with me. None of it made sense.

In my uncertainty, I asked my friend and fellow student Sagar Malde, a tall, wiry Kenyan Indian kid with a beautiful accent whose father owned the entire East African soap industry.

Sagar exclaimed, "Of course they know!" like it was obvious. "They know your exam results."

The response didn't solve the mystery. As far as I knew, my results were good, but they weren't public and weren't the greatest in the university. Sagar did much better than me.

When I asked, "Of course, Gary," he answered sweetly, "but no one expects that from you."

Sagar was a nice boy; we're still friends. But I was astonished then. Since childhood, I've been good at numbers. Everyone in primary and high school knew I was strong at arithmetic. I occasionally entered competitions and usually won. My teachers, family, and friends expected it. Always expected it from myself. Though jealous, no one was surprised.

However, Sagar's offhand comment made me understand something I had never considered before: rich people believe poor people to be foolish. The LSE first-year economics seminars draw about 1,000 students. I appeared to those wealthier students as a bit of fun but not a threat by sitting in the front row during those lectures, wearing a tracksuit and carrying a Nike string backpack, and asking questions with an East London accent. My freshman year results were shocking. I mulled it over and wondered what to do. I resolved then to prove that tracksuit kids aren't stupid. I didn't know what a CDS was, but I could do math. Yes, we'll show them. Show them what we can do.

While everyone else applied to thirty-seven investment banks, I lavishly demonstrated my economics and math skills to anyone who would listen. I began studying in my spare time for the first time. I asked the lecturers more questions. I challenged them when they erred. To be honest, I didn't know if or how it would lead to a profession, but I wasn't worrying about it anymore. Just let them know they weren't superior to us. Because they're not.

Some strange incident happened one day. A gangly Grimsby kid with thick black hair and a muddled business suit approached me in the library. Luke Blackwood was my math classmate last year.

In response to his question, I said I was Gary.

Listen, Citibank has an event next week. Though named "The Trading Game," it's a math game. By winning, you can advance to the national final and gain an internship. I heard you're good at math. Get going."

Luke sat next to me, informed me of the competition's date and time, and briefly discussed the regulations. I had never met him before. Luke stated trading was a basic mathematical game, so I didn't have to know anything about it. After explaining everything, Luke stood up and left, leaving me with a blinking computer and a few half-finished arithmetic assignment pages on A4.

I was sure I would win that game right away, maybe because I was brash and overconfident. Despite not knowing about CDSs, CDOs, or Asset Backed Securities, I knew about games and math. I thought this was finally a way into the City without playing the oboe. Finally, a level playing field and real competition. I knew I could win. I put my textbooks and math homework aside. I calculated all the game math on a spreadsheet.

***

The first Trading Game round began a few days following my talk with Luke. I had only attended two finance events. I hadn't seen the game advertised, but a medium-sized queue snaked out of one of LSE's enormous office block buildings on a balmy fall evening. A multinational mix of Chinese, Russians, Pakistanis, and others whose accents and clothing spoke more of trust funds than any nationality.

I knew I had an advantage over them. I had the game rules explained, but they hadn't. That was unfair, but life is. God knows these people had plenty of regulations presented to them that I would never know. It felt like my first advantage. I liked feeling my fingers and toes vibrate as the queue moved in.

The line of eager, young aspiring traders poured into a big, high-ceilinged, windowless lecture theater in the building's basement, which I had never seen before. Our five-person groups were arranged on separate tables. A massive man shone in front of a flip chart at the front of the room. First time seeing a trader. Then a trader must look like that, I thought.

The trader explained the regulations when we sat down. Naturally, I knew the rules, so I could watch him speak. He moved slowly and decisively around the room. He smiled confidently and looked at each kid in the throng with bright eyes. Confidence appeared to seep from him like candle smoke into the room. It had a thick, sticky darkness, a sharp, glittering brightness like treacle in a glass jar, and that gigantic, never-ending, pearly white smile. That dark, sticky certainty took me back to Ilford. Bag sales made £10 into £100 for cool school kids turned drug traffickers. I hadn't seen such depth in Ilford. Something I noticed at LSE. A winner's confidence today and tomorrow. He knows he can't lose. Even though I understood nothing about trading, I felt it was meant for me.

However, work must be done first. My competition was to win.

And how would I do that? You must first comprehend the game.

The trade game was a numbers game, not a simulation.

The unusual deck had seventeen numbered cards, some higher and others lower. In case you wish to play, the whole deck had a -10, a 20, and all the digits 1 through 15. Each player sees their card, then three more are placed face-down in the center of the table. The game involves participants betting on the total numerical value of the eight cards (five players each have one card, plus the three in the middle).

Imagine that you're all buying and selling an asset worth the sum of the cards in the game. As the game progresses, the middle cards give more information than your card. A high card like the 15, or 20, tells you the total will be high, therefore you want to make "buy" bets. Make "sell" bets on low totals with a low card like -10. A 6 or 7 middle card means you'll have to create something up.

The betting mechanism was supposed to simulate "price-making" and "price-taking" in "two-way markets," making the game a "trading game."

Let me just explain financial market trading. Big customers like pension funds, hedge funds, and corporations seek to acquire or sell. They could buy anything, but let's say ten million British pounds for US dollars. They rarely phone banks to claim, "Hi there, I want to buy ten million British pounds in exchange for USD." Two reasons they don't:

1. If the trader knows you want to buy British pounds, he's probably going to try and push the price of pounds up.

2. If the trader knows you want to buy British pounds, he could even go out into the market and quickly buy loads of pounds, in the hope of pushing the market price up before selling them to you at that higher price. This is called "frontrunning" and is, in many cases, illegal, but it happens a lot.

To clarify, customers should not inform traders they want to buy before they can. To avoid this, say, "Hi, give me a price of ten million pounds."

In principle, the trader won't know if you wish to purchase or sell. The convention is that he must give you two prices—buy and sell. Most significant financial markets use a "two-way price" system. Similar to the currency counter at an airport, it has one price to buy pounds for dollars and another to sell pounds for dollars. Naturally, they acquire for far less than they sell. That's how forex counters make money. The same happens with traders.

Citibank's Trading Game worked similarly. Any player can inquire "what's your price?" and the other player must answer a two-way price with a 2-point margin.

Imagine you're an LSE student playing this game as a young, money-hungry trader. You sit at a table wearing an expensive suit your dad, a Chinese Politburo member, got from London's best tailor. A large, confident-looking man briefly explains the rules of a simple maths game, and then a small, aggressive-looking boy with an almost incomprehensible accent and a white hoodie with a blue rhino asks, "What's your price?"

You do what?

The answer is evident for most LSE students with economics, math, and statistics backgrounds. Looking at your hand and the possible cards in the deck, you calculate the "expected value" of the whole sum using a basic statistical computation. Not a hard math calculation. The average deck card value is 7.65. The average score should be 61.2 if there are eight cards. If you know one of the cards, you will adjust the total based on its high or low value. Expect 68 with a 20. Since 20 is 12 more than 7.65, you might have expected 73, but having 20 means no one else has 20, thus it only raises the expectation by 7. Expect 51.2 with a -10.

The math is straightforward and easy. It worked for everyone at the table.

It's stupid. I'll explain why.

I had studied LSE maths, economics, and finance for a year. I know their thinking and expected this. Imagine playing this game. Imagine one person at your table has the 20 and quotes 67–69 immediately (his expectation is 68). Another individual quotes 50–52 with the -10. What do you do?

You know immediately that one guy has the -10 and the other the 20. They showed you their cards with their first words. That's beside the point. You can bet that the 50–52 guy's total will be higher than 52. You can then wager with the 67–69 person that the total will be below 67. Buy 52, sell 67. Two bets cancel out immediately, giving you a 15 profit. A risk-free profit of 15 regardless of the game total. Do it again. If the other participants are smart, they'll notice your quick profit. They will learn that selling something for 52 while another man wants to purchase it at 67 is ridiculous. Smart gamers will see that the small child with the rhino sweatshirt has asked for 15 prices in the first minute and made 100 guaranteed. They'll realize he may be right. They may consider adjusting.

But LSE Economics students and Finance Society attendees are stupid. Different kinds of intelligence. They use calculators and spreadsheets well. In a room with a Deutsche Bank recruiter and a good tie and wine, they may make lively conversation. Make them play a card game with a quick-talking East London lad who has had three days to figure it out. They won't know they're losing until it's an hour late.

Suddenly, I won the tournament. Repeatedly purchase low and sell high. It was ludicrous. Other players barely looked up from their calculators. I was throwing points into the bag while they calculated their predicted values.

Although it was a math game, it taught us about markets:

1. Individual traders don't set the price. Just because you think something is worth 60, you don't offer to buy it at 59 if everyone else is selling it at 50. If other people are selling it at 50, the highest you should possibly quote is 50–52. There is no point offering to buy at 51 if someone is out there selling at 50.

This shows something interesting about markets, which is that an individual trader shouldn't quote what they think something is worth, but rather what everyone else thinks is the price.

2. Because of this, if you ask ten different traders for a price, you shouldn't get ten different prices: they should all converge on a similar price. This will be true even if the ten different traders have totally different views about what the price should actually be.

3. If another guy looks like he knows what he's doing and is making a load of money, and you have no clue what you are doing, then maybe you should just copy that guy.

4. Point 3 is the main driver in most financial markets.

I know the first trading competition round was unfair. I learned the regulations three days in advance, but everyone else learned them that day. That probably helped me win that game. That was the first step to securing a job that would make me a millionaire. I realize that wasn't fair. Personally, I don't care. The remainder of those guys in that room were millionaires because their dads were. Some traders became traders because their fathers were traders. My dad worked for the Post Office, so I didn't have a mathematical desk at home. I suppose you take breaks where you can. I shook the trader's enormous hand at the front of the room.

"Well done," he said. "See you in the final."

"Thanks," I said. "See you there."

***

I scarcely attended a lecture or lesson between the LSE round of the trading game and the national final, which lasted three weeks. Matic also survived. I taught all my pals how to play and hid in a library room for three weeks, playing with everyone who would join. I memorised spreadsheets of the game when I couldn't find somebody to play it with. A Citibank employee dreamed up this ridiculous numbers game. I must have been the world's foremost specialist by the final.

In 2006, the Citigroup skyscraper, HSBC Tower, and blinking pyramid dome of Canary Wharf skyscraper formed the triangle of the country's three highest buildings, where the final was held. I had noticed those skyscrapers on the horizon from Ilford, between the street lamp poles. This seemed fateful. But I had to win.

Cold early winter replaced warm early fall by the final. Wearing a dark blue checkered shirt with a large blue-and-yellow tie. At DFS, I wore it with fluff pillows. I took the tube from the LSE to Canary Wharf in the gloomy afternoon. The Jubilee Line trains sounded nothing like the ones that passed my bed every morning. When they accelerate and decelerate, they swirl, whirr, and climb. They sounded new. Their sound was high-tech. Always sounded like money to me.

The tower's top floor hosted the game. The winter nighttime view from that height shows London as a jumble of windows and lamp poles. As a child, I looked at these skyscrapers daily. One day, I might have tried to see my house through the windows. Rather than sightseeing, my head was full with numbers. Besides, I wouldn't have known which direction to look.

A champagne and canapé reception preceded the game. Not drinking champagne or knowing what a canapé was. Other candidates spoke and laughed with merchants. Perhaps giggling about CDOs. But I didn't listen. I came for the stats. Five competitors from LSE, Oxford, Cambridge, Durham, and Warwick advanced. Citibank probably didn't care about other universities. Twenty-five competitors, including me, and I played with all the LSE players. I Like my chances.

We sat at tables. I assessed my opponents as the huge, smiling trader from the first round at LSE gave some inspiring comments. I must change my plan for this round. Everyone had played well enough in the opening round to advance. They should have known that quoting prices that differed from others is absurd. Thus, buying low and selling high between participants would not yield easy profits.

However, that players would recognize the folly of quoting widely apart presented fresh opportunities. Through my continuous practice games, I saw that most players stuck closely to the pricing listed around them, deviating just slightly. They mostly listened to quoted pricing to keep their own costs close. This allowed me to control prices by publicly quoting them myself. The game was free-for-all, like actual markets, and loudly reciting 58–60 would often lower prices around 62–64. Another way to set the price is to loudly quote a price at the start of the game.

This offered an innovative, potentially profitable strategy. With a high card, I would call out a low price to start. This is a basic bluff—indicating that I have a low card to lower the price so I can buy at a low level from multiple players since everyone has stuck to my initial cheap price. This may lead to other players realizing I was bluffing, buying from me at a low price, and trading at a high price. I relied on my friend Sagar Malde's simple lesson from weeks earlier: rich people believe poor people to be ignorant. If someone who looks and talks like me opens the game by loudly declaring an unusually low price, the other players are more likely to see it as a simpleton showing his hand cheaply than a bluff.

After that, they would constantly inquire about pricing to figure out their strategy and hands. I was using another piece of information from the LSE players: most of them were hoping to network at the final rather than win the competition. Most players would quote slightly higher than the average if they had a high card and slightly lower if they had a bad card. Rarely did sellers quote a neutral price to conceal information. Few ever bluff. Remember, they are economics students, not poker players.

The upshot is that modern economists are mathematicians, not intellectuals or gamers. I guided their ears and read their gaze as the other pupils played with calculators. Start with a loud bluff, then quickly examine each player's intelligence, complexity, and likely card. After that, I'd determine whether to buy (bet the total will be high) or sell. If I was a buyer, I openly quoted low prices and bought from other players at that level. If I sold, I did the opposite.

The method worked perfectly, and after five games, I advanced to the final. Five players remain. One internship at risk. The odds are good. When the five of us proceeded to the central table, the eliminated competitors grabbed canapés and watched.

Sized up the players surrounding me. I played most of them before this final. They were all good, fast to pick up on price swings and mathematically informed, but none of them seemed smart enough to bluff or read bluffing. I thought my odds were good.

Cards came up and I got -10. Good card. The -10 has the most power to affect the game total because it is farthest from the average. However, it's only useful if others don't know you have it. Otherwise, they'll instantly decrease their pricing, leaving you little profit. Another trading rule: you gain money by being correct when others are wrong.

My customary technique was to immediately set a high price. If I could set a high price throughout the game, I could "sell" at high prices and maximize my -10 card.

Although I paid a lot, the first player did not "sell" to me. For his price, I inquired. Even higher. He's showing off–he has a high card.

I asked the other three players. All quoted excessive pricing. Everyone looked to have good cards. That meant we would have a high total, not including my -10, so I had to raise the price to make a profit. I kept quoting higher and louder until folks sold to me. I raised the price and sold aggressively. The -10 in my hand made it nearly hard to lose at this price. I would quote my prices loudly, pushing the market up as if I were an active buyer, but then sell when asked for other players' bids. In the turmoil and cacophony of the game, other participants couldn't keep track of who was buying and selling from their quoted prices, but the repeated numbers had a tremendous influence on the price.

I started accumulating "sell" bets, knowing that the eventual total would be much lower at this price. Time to flip the first of the three core cards. It was 13.

A 13 hurt me. It increases the projected card total by 3 points due to its greater value than 7.65. This was bad news because my scorecard included many "sell" bets. I held the -10, which nobody knew about, and prices were high. All maths went my way. I increased the price and kept selling. I had two complete sell bet scorecards by the second card. The second card was 14.

It was probably time to be skeptical, but I wasn't. No time to be. I needed a low total or my career was over, but I wouldn't stop if it wasn't. I raised the price and sold more aggressively. I sold 300 times by the end of the game's end.

Last card went over. It was 20. Four more players flipped their cards. 10, 11, 12, 15. It was impossible. Except for my -10 card, the other cards were the game's seven highest. One in eleven thousand, four hundred and forty chances. 0:0087%. The game was fixed. I had no idea what to do. I felt cold for a time. The Audience enjoyed it. Naturally, other players were excited. My scorecards were always full of buys since I sold so much. The price was exorbitant. Game-rigged by whom? Why? This might signify what?

As traders and Citigroup personnel counted scores in the rear of the room, the table disbanded. Players blended into the crowd.

"Sorry mate." Matic held my shoulder. That was an unlucky mate. You did well."

I don't remember what I told Matic. Maybe I said nothing.

Room seemed to melt for five minutes. I held a flute of champagne with those small bubbles that kept popping up and soaring skyward. What just happened? Who did it? They'd cheat me why?

Soon later, the trader entered the center of the room, calming the crowd with his size. The space expanded around him.

He said, "I would like to thank you all for playing," and his strong American voice drew me back to the room. "We calculated the scores, and I can announce the winner."

Someone's score is forgotten. But mine was under - 1,000. This is not good. No, I wasn't humiliated. You don't score without shooting.

The heavy-set trader pronounced the winner after perusing the scores. He called my name. Victory was mine. It was me.

In a daze, I advanced. The trader spoke to the audience while shaking my hand. We tested Gary since his warm-up ratings were so high. We set up the game to see how he reacted when everything went wrong. Knowing if a trader will back down is crucial. Gary, you supported yourself, which we appreciate. Well done."

The trader extended his enormous hand again, and I grabbed it.

I'm Caleb Zucman, see you at the desk."

***

That night, I drank in the park with friends despite the cold. I was intoxicated and don't remember anything. One recollection sticks out. I remember moving rapidly and feeling chilly air sweep across my face. That memory shows me holding a friend's shoulders. "I'll be a millionaire!" I shout. He laughs while I yell at him. "I'll be a millionaire!"

PART TWO
YOU WANT SOME?

1

The summer internship came from that March STIRT desk week. Everyone recognized me as the youngster who bought them burgers when I arrived. That stunt showed everyone Caleb wanted me, so everyone wanted me. Caleb wanted me more after the Credit Trading desk pushed me. Everything was done despite, or rather without regard for, the fact that I still had no notion what anyone was doing. This may be called a "speculative bubble," and if you think about it, you can learn how bitcoin works.

The through line was visible. I smelled everywhere. I had killed my end-of-year tests. I would savage the summer internship. After graduating, I was offered a full-time job a year later. I would reach that, become the world's top trader, and become a millionaire. My plan was incomplete, like my lack of trading skills, but I was fucked if I allowed it stop me. Screaming killed that year.

I concentrated on winning all internship competitions that summer. I won all three "trading competitions". All had little tricks you could exploit if you knew them. They ended up playing games. I won a public speaking contest. I have no idea what to say about that. I guess I was a competitive youngster.

Matic also interned at Citi. He must have networked during the trading game final. He was adept. A super-high-tech-futuristic-massive-spreadsheet-million-formula desk called "Credit Structuring" had him fucked up on coffee and caffeine pills for the entire internship. They were World Gods then. Matic rarely went home throughout the internship. He spent all day buzzing on Microsoft Excel and slept under the desk at night. He used to set an alarm for 5 a.m. to wake up before anyone else and hide his overnight stay. After the internship, Citi offered him a full-time job, but he chose Cambridge for his Computer Science Master's. He interned again the following summer. Some folks are nuts, I think.

After everyone went home, I sat with Matic as he did his spreadsheets. He was tall and strong, but his mouse and keyboard hands shook slightly as his sleepy eyes darted around.

I asked Matic what to do with my newfound notoriety at one of those conversations.

Matic stated, "Don't work on the STIRT desk." He called traders "anachronisms" "stuck in the eighties." Despite my disinterest, Matic's statement that "FX traders don't make any money" was more concerning.

"FX" refers to "Foreign Exchange," while STIRT is for "Short Term Interest Rates Trading," yet it's in the Foreign Exchange sector. The genius-credit-trader side of the trading floor thought FX traders were fools and that computers would replace them. There was no future. They literally called FX traders "monkeys," a label they happily adopted. The scathing accusation that they were poor was more damaging and hurtful. That was my sole concern.

However, for reasons I couldn't explain, I guess I'd already decided. I left Matic with a Red Bull or coffee after such chats. I fucked off and he slept on the floor.

***

As expected, I was offered a full-time position on the Citi grad plan after the internship, and the STIRT boys kept an eye on me when I returned to LSE for my final year. Each of them believed they would have been professional athletes if not for some unfortunate teenage injury or other cruel twist of fate, and my introduction had finally given them access to the numbers needed for a regular football game: no matter how many we were short, I could always pull some kids up from the street back in Ilford who'd be up for a free game and a couple of beers. I saw most STIRT guys every week for football. The best players were Hongo and, oddly, Scouse Billy, running around with his round belly. Always knew Rupert was behind you when playing. He growled in your ear.

Caleb and Rupert watched me closely and made several overtures during the year. I thought they were coordinated, but I later learned the two men loathed each other and made competitive bids.

Rupert hired me and some street kids to paint his Clapham flat. He offered to pay us £100 per day, even if I'm no painter. He gave me £50 bills I couldn't spend. After three fifty-dollar attempts to buy moisturizer from Boots, I gave up and went home. Rupert's apartment was huge. A cinema floor located on the bottom of three storeys. Only the bathrooms had doors in the flat. Everyone else had rotating walls. Despite being white, he wanted us to paint the flat white. Whatever. I believed it was his money.

It was probably April when Caleb called me in and sat me down in a little glass-walled office with a view of the other small offices on the other side of the dock.

Today, huge investment banks don't tell you what role you'll play. You have to do this big "graduate scheme" training/rotation program where they teach you nonsense nobody cares about in classrooms on the top floor, then you spend a year and a half rotating around trading floor desks hoping someone will hire you.

Caleb opposed that. Start straight on the desk, he said. He made me two distinct offers, but I don't know if he understood I didn't like the desk. Number one: I could start whenever. Number two: I could trade immediately. That meant a profit-and-loss spreadsheet line with my name and a figure. That's how folks get compensated. Clear cash by your name. Getting that normally takes years.

Perhaps that's why I chose the STIRT desk despite Matic's advice. Perhaps in my boyish, twenty-one-year-old overconfidence, I knew that if they handed me a line on the profit-and-loss spreadsheet, it would be the bank's biggest within years. It would have been accurate. It might not have been. It could have been Billy's Scouse accent and JB's rugby stories. It could have been Rupert's revolving walls in his cinema room. Or maybe it was the way Caleb stared at me in that small glass box that sunny April afternoon, with that wide smile and his eyes glittering like the sea I could see through the window in the wharf.

***

My latest LSE exam was "MA303: Chaos in Dynamical Systems." Thursday, June 26, 2008. I told Caleb I'd start Monday. This weekend I need to buy pants and shirts.

Hobbs took me to LA and Vegas after Caleb talked. One of the traders suffered a nosebleed in a limousine on the way to Carmen Electra's birthday celebration. I believed it was the altitude, so I gave him a tissue. He declined. I wore a £20 H&M gray waistcoat.

I was meant to study for tests.

***

There I was. I'm 21 with freshly shaved hair and Topman sharp shoes. I entered the trading floor on June 30, 2008, the youngest trader in the City, four days after my last university exam. No idea why I shaved my head. Making the decision felt perfect.

I recall gathering all my business cards and sending everyone a handwritten thank-you email after my first one-week internship a year

23

and a half earlier. I asked for advice and reading suggestions for my new career in those emails.

The scary-eyed middle-aged Englishman Clarky emailed me a short, harsh reply. It only said:

It was nice to meet you, Gary. Don't rush the trading floor. Take Your time, see the world, enjoy your youth. Once you get in, you'll never get out.

All the best,

Clarky

***

Well, I hadn't heard of Clarky. I now think it was smarter advice. Why didn't I accept?

I remember being hungry as a twenty-one-year-old. I was probably hungry for a while. Sleeping on broken beds does that. Know what I mean? Do you?

If you wanted to rob a bank and saw the vault door open, what would you do? Would you wait?

How will you see the world without money?

It was my time to shine, man.

***

I knew things would be different from day one. This was no longer just "impress the boys—buy some burgers—get a job." There's a profit-and-loss line next to my name now. That's my money. Money for me.

So what do we do? There's a double-pronged plan of attack.

1. Learn to trade.
2. Get a book.

Easy plan, right? What's a book?

Everyone on the STIRT desk trades FX swaps. Never fear if you don't understand an FX swap. I was also unsure. It's enough to know that you can trade an FX swap in any currency, and the STIRT desk traded ten currencies—EUR, GBP, CHF, SEK, NOK, DKK, JPY, and AUD, NZD, CAD—against the US dollar.

Every trader handles one or more currencies. Rupert was the senior euro trader, sharing a "book" with Ho Nguyen. Bill oversaw the British pound book. Caleb managed the Swiss currency, while JB handled the AUD, NZD, and yen.

So why is a book important?

A book is important because it brings all clients and deals in a currency straight to you. Why's it good?

Remember the trade game lesson. Anyone can ask for a price at any moment and must use a "two-point-spread." For instance, "I will buy at 67 or I will sell at 69." Imagine the game had outside consumers willing to trade on a larger spread, such as the four-point spread 66–70, meaning "I will buy at 66 or I will sell at 70." That resembles real markets. If that happened, you could buy from outside buyers at 66 and sell it for 67, making a guaranteed profit of 1. If you held onto the risk longer, you might find someone prepared to pay 68 or 69, doubling or tripling your profit. So "getting a book" means that. Access to consumers prepared to trade at below-market prices means practically guaranteed profit for you, which you surely already know is a good thing. If you think about it, Thomas Cook does this to your foreign currency money every time you go on vacation.

Why are customers prepared to trade below market prices? That's an excellent question, but I didn't ask it at 21. No worries, though. Be patient.

For now, book acquisition.

The downside of free money is that you must be ready to set prices at any time once you have a book. Sometimes someone needs an FX swap in Swiss francs, Australian dollars, or whatever fuck book you trade. Citibank offers 24-hour pricing (with desks in New York, Sydney, and Tokyo), so if you're pissed or in Las Vegas, someone makes that price. Everyone on the desk had a partner who made the price if they were off the desk or incapacitated (certain traders were incapacitated more often than others, as we'll discover).

This employment, "cover trader," is crucial. If you are off the desk and the cover trader offers a price in your currency, the trade goes in your book and you profit (or lose). As a junior trader, cover trading was crucial. The senior traders on the desk could profit or lose. You might demonstrate price-making trading. You could claim your own book. If you could prove you were a good or profitable cover trader, senior traders would fight for you when they were away. This would quickly show everyone that you were rightly next in line for a book and may have reminded the bossmen that the tired-looking, graying trader in the corner didn't need to run three books to himself.

Green people aren't wanted as cover. You're dangerous. A liability, you. Trust must be earned first. The two aims meet here. Develop trust, demonstrate your cover trading skills, and ideally they'll teach you to trade.

We need a mark again. Analyze our choices.

Billy is the obvious pick. Bill has become a legend in my eyes and has been named the smartest trader on the desk by Snoopy, whom I respect. Additionally, he is British, short, and not a pompous dickhead. We have a lot in common. That may work. Only thing is, when I get to the desk, Snoopy has relocated into that area and claimed it. Snoopy is a year and a half older and experienced. That will be hard to get.

Rupert and JB are clear next. I've impressed both guys, and they seem eager to work with me. I might get in with either, but there are issues. The most obvious is that they both seem nuts. JB first. JB is a great person, and I've heard all his stories and had many beers with him. I spent five weeks at this desk during my summer internship. He speaks at a million miles an hour, so I don't grasp anything he says about trading or anything else. He may not be a good spiritual leader. Also, a young Frankenstein-looking trader from New York is sitting next to JB. That slot could be taken too.

That leaves Rupert. Here, the pros are evident. First, he took me to Vegas. Second, I decorated his bedroom. That seems like a decent friendship foundation, right? Rupert and Hongo divide the euro book, although Hong is in his 30s and there's room for a junior. As the desk's largest trader, the senior euro rates trader must be good, and his logical, disciplined trading technique could be a good model to emulate. He may be a psychopath. I've spent enough time with him to know that's risky. Nobody's perfect, right?

Naturally, Caleb existed. Always Caleb. Caleb is the boss. That's impossible—I'm no teacher's pet.

So I chose Rupert. Rupert chose me.

When Snoopy moved to Billy's corner by the window, I was put in his old seat, far from the window, half overflowing into the aisle. The vacant station to my left separated me from most traders. It's unclear why this station was always unoccupied. Perhaps it was a physical reminder to me and Snoopy that desk juniors should know their place. Rupert was to the left of that empty spot and ignored me for half my first day.

When I returned from lunch at 2 p.m., Rupert was sitting in the vacant swivel chair next to mine and swinging it. That scared me, but I pretended nothing was wrong. It was hard to ignore him when I sat down and gazed straight ahead into my screens. Both of his large round knees were pointed at me.

"Where have you been?"

I turned to him like nothing was wrong. The fuck was squeezed from a neon-orange stress ball.

I went to lunch?

What did you eat? Rupert answered before I could mark my inquiry.

"It was like sausage, beans, and tomatoes?"

"Where did you get that?"

"Erm… The downstairs canteen gave it to me."

Rupert was silent again and staring at me for too long, which would have been embarrassing for everyone save me and him.

I've worked at this desk for 12 years. I've never visited that canteen. We eat. On the desk."

Then he stared at me for a while, and I didn't know what to say.

Two months earlier, Rupert and I were standing by a pool on a warm, dark evening at Jay-Z's LA afterparty. Rupert asked a gorgeous yellow bikini-clad girl her Chinese zodiac sign. BTW, Rupert was a tiger. So was I.

What was the girl? I forget.

OK, I thought. So it will be, right?

No issue.

***

Not an isolated instance. Rupert began to grab me from behind and shout things like "WHAT IS UK CONSUMER CONFIDENCE?" during my first few days, when I was mostly installing software and talking to Jimmy John in Bangalore.

What is the US Services PMI?

I knew the right answer was "I don't know." Sadly, that wasn't enough anymore.

"That's no longer acceptable Gary! You trade now! Knowing is essential!"

This was upsetting for several reasons. First, the "I don't know" method had been so successful throughout my internship that losing it was like losing a leg. Second, I didn't even know what PMI meant. Three-letter acronyms have always been my weakness. After being forcibly dragged from my seat during a long-distance call, I panicked and exclaimed, "Forty-seven point one!"

A guess.

The answer may have been righteous fury, and because the number shouted was inaccurate and made up (never a good combo), it was probably reasonable.

I did two things for my nerves.

First, I sneaked up to Snoopy and asked him what a PMI was and how I might get its daily amount.

Snoopy showed me a "Economic Release Calendar," which lists all the economic data released worldwide, every day, and its exact time. Daily data points can exceed fifty or sixty, but they are usually issued all at once for each country, so there are only three or four significant periods. I started checking the data release times every morning and setting alarms on my Nokia phone five minutes in advance. I never got a number wrong after that, and Rupert stopped groping me after two weeks. What a relief. I kept setting those alarms every weekday for

28

three years after that. By then, I didn't care about data releases, and no one would have grabbed me.

That was a long time ago, but sometimes when I'm at my laptop and not focused, I open that calendar. UK Inputs Producer Price Inflation was released at 7 a.m. today. It was 22.6%. Pretty high.

Second, I resolved that I would not learn to trade from Rupert Hobhouse if there was any other option.

2

`So I got Spengler.

Theodore Barnaby Spengler III was a fool.

Actually, that's probably unfair. He was more idiot-savant.

Spengler was not my mentor of choice. He was not my second or third. After deciding to escape Rupert, I tried Bill. After convincing him to let me manually enter some of his trades into the computer systems, I made a mistake in my first week and he screamed "You cost me forty FUCKING grand you fucking TWAT!" halfway across the floor.

$40k was twice my dad's salary. With my tail between my legs, I returned to my final safe haven and rolled my swivel chair next to JB, just like on my first day at the desk.

JB now had Theodore Spengler's Frankenstein-like frame next to him. I saw Theodore Spengler's gurning, bobbing head next to JB's the first time I returned to the desk as a full-time hire. He looked like Herman Munster from the Munsters. The winter before, Caleb fired three traders. I thought Spengler was a rising talent hired to replace them.

I rapidly realized otherwise.

Spengler had been hired by the New York STIRT desk from the US graduation program approximately a year earlier. They quickly realized this was a terrible mistake and urged Caleb to take him off their hands. What Caleb got for that cursed present is unknown, but I hope it was good.

What was wrong with the boy?

Spengler, a large, lumbering muffin-shaped man, walked like a farmer falling over. His arrival at the counter was precisely 7:29 a.m., one minute before being late. He always turned on a speakerbox switch and called a broker after sitting down. The broker, with a familiar name ending in y, would call out names like "Hey Granty!", "Hey Millsy!", or "Hey Johnathan!"

He spoke in an incomprehensible accent because he was from Johannesburg or Cape Town.

The broker, usually from Essex or East London, would respond with "Hey Spengler!" How are you doing, old rogue/big charmer/maniac? Last night was insane! Did you get home okay?

I discovered on one of my first mornings with Spengler that he had pissed himself in a taxi on the way home. He informed his broker frankly and joyfully. The broker laughed at it, which surprised me because it was terrible. JB looked over his shoulder at Spengler, confirming my feelings.

I forget which broker Spengler recounted this story to. It was probably Granty. It doesn't matter since Spengler then turned up each switch one by one and told seven brokers the same narrative in the same words. All brokers, including the three Danish Carstens, laughed hilariously. The process took 30 minutes total. I discovered brokers are paid to chuckle.

Spengler had other misdeeds outside public hygiene. He would tell me bad jokes nonstop. JB always chastised him for inappropriate jokes. That didn't slow the child, who seemed to enjoy ridicule. Any time JB chastised him, the boy's pained gurn would stretch and his dull eyes would twinkle, shine, or smile.

Some jokes were anti-Semitic. A foolish move for a South African behemoth sitting three meters from a Jewish employer who can set his compensation. When he made one of these jokes when Caleb was walking behind him, Caleb grabbed the back of his swivel chair and spun him 180 degrees. Caleb said nothing but peered down at the youngster, who looked up at the guy who was just three years older than him and looked deep into his eyes. His mouth seemed to be trying to form words, but he said nothing and suddenly closed his lips. He seemed ready to suck his thumb. After 15 seconds, Caleb groaned and turned Spengler's chair around and left grumbling.

"Think about what the fuck you are doing you retard."

Spengler would itch his arse and eat burgers too fast. More importantly, I remember Spengler's calls to his mother. The boy's mother called daily at 3 p.m. Unexpectedly, they spoke Flemish for an hour. Even today, I'm glad I don't speak Flemish.

The worst part was I loved the boy.

Why?

Probably because he was a great dealer.

***

Brokers, what are they?

People may use "broker" and "trader" interchangeably. They are very distinct universes. Even at this time, it felt like most brokers were from Essex or East London, even though the trading floor was in East London and had no such accents.

As Rupert so aptly stated, the differences went beyond language. Without an "elite" degree, trading floors were nearly inaccessible by 2008. Every trader on the STIRT desk, including me, had one except Bill. The majority of brokers had never attended college.

Brokers' cockney voices echo from desk speaker boxes. In a cadence reminiscent of fruit and vegetable street markets, their dulcet voices chant numbers repeatedly. One-pound strawberries, three-month euros, 4.3 4.6. Since I last worked on a London trading floor nearly ten years ago, I wonder if those melodious voices are still so cockney. I hope so, but I doubt it.

Brokers aren't bank employees. The cartels dubbed "brokerages" employ them to link merchants. Brokers simply match trades made by traders. Importantly, traders bear the risk of failed deals, not brokers. Brokers resemble estate agents. They work on commission, therefore they want you to make more deals regardless of quality.

In theory, brokers let you buy without alerting your opponents. This is useful for huge players like Citibank who want to acquire without moving the market. Suppose you want to buy something for 36, you tell your broker, and he shouts "36 bid 36 bid 36 bid" down every speakerbox in the City, hoping to find a seller. You can buy without anyone knowing, which is beneficial since if they know you want to buy, they may raise the price before you can.

But that's the theory. What's real?

Broker lunches are a reality.

***

Back in the cab with Rupert, we arrived at a classy Central London restaurant. I wish I could tell you the place's name, but I don't.

It was a Japanese restaurant, and an immaculate hostess in an amazing costume greeted us in a small but impeccable reception space that was too gloomy for the time of day. Dazzled by all the magnificence, I was escorted up or down stairs into a spacious dining room that was both bright from huge windows and strangely dark due to all the black furniture.

Before midday, the massive, jet-black, perfectly spherical, alien-looking tables were practically vacant. After a long tour of the large dining space, the hostess led us around a glass bottle wall. This took us to a private room where the largest and blackest table was flooded in sunlight next to a floor-to-ceiling window that shed a harsh slanted light on three brokers sitting huddled on the table's far side.

The three brokers stood up at once and rushed to shake our hands when we entered.

I measured the three. Young was rude and confused. Middle-aged, sensuous, serpentine. And an older one, with thick, pure white hair, who must have been at least sixty years old and looked like his head had never stopped growing.

The person with the large head introduced himself with a deep voice: "Hi, my name is Bighead."

Of course, the h is unpronounced.

A dance followed as the five of us struggled to fit comfortably around the huge round table. It was hard, and I ended up on the other side of the table, next to Bighead, who reminded me of my dead grandad with his deep cockney accent, thick shock of impossibly white hair, and pure size. It also meant I wasn't next to Rupert. I appreciated that the talk flowed like a river from the brokers to Rupert since I didn't have to say anything and had time to observe.

Although Bighead was the oldest, he did not lead the discourse. Timothy Twineham, a middle-aged trader with thick, unnaturally black hair, did that. Conversation was flawless. Tasted like honey. No break or pause. To add drama, Bighead would fill gaps with his contrabass voice. Sitting between Timothy and Rupert, the young trader said nothing. He alternated between the two like a tennis match, nodding excitedly and occasionally rocking his face backward for a cackling laugh.

I giggled softly as the young broker did that. Rupert never laughed.

White wine and a huge sashimi dish were provided. I didn't know what sashimi was. It's riceless sushi. Sashimi is healthier than sushi and can help you lose weight, Rupert told me (with some difficulty, given we were far apart) I seized Rupert and the platter. I nodded profoundly. I used a clean chopstick to spear a small, pinkish-white fish into the middle of the table and try to balance it on my plate.

I drank white wine rapidly, even though I don't enjoy it, to avoid making a mistake. The background music was an anonymous deep bassy music that I have since found to be almost ubiquitous in expensive London restaurants. After a while, the music, wine, and conversation started to blend together, and I could barely hear anyone. Nevermind—I didn't have to say anything. My job was to lean forward into the table, look intensely at the speaker, and sometimes nod off into the distance. Rupert taught me the chopstick method, but I dropped three fish on the table and one on the floor.

The second course took a while. I was getting intoxicated by then and had some technical issues with the first course, mostly because it was slick and far away.

Unfortunately, the second meal was a huge plate of raw chicken and beef. You probably know that raw chicken is unsafe to eat, and I suspected so too. I had a similar strong belief about raw fish till an hour earlier, which turned out to be inaccurate. Eventually, I gave up after waiting a few minutes to see what others were doing because they were talking about the Morgan Stanley Senior Euro Dealer. I finally placed a piece of raw chicken between two sticks on my plate without contamination. I ate it. It was revolting.

The disgustingness made me rethink this Japanese ritual, so I poked Bighead, with whom I was swiftly building an unsaid, grand-paternal bond, under the table.

He leaned toward me conspiratorially.

I whispered, "Don't you think this chicken is…A little…Disgusting??"

Bighead, who had drunk a lot of wine, looked at me curiously. After viewing the enormous meat and chicken tray, he turned and stared at me.

"Did you eat chicken?" He seemed confused.

I ate it because it's chicken. What the hell else should I do?

My new grandad laughed deeply and loudly and stood up and removed a part of the table, and wow, there was a whole fucking grill under there and nobody had told me. He laughed for ages, and nobody understood why because he didn't tell anyone that I'd eaten raw chicken, which I was grateful for.

No one paid for that lunch two hours later.

Someone must have paid, but I didn't see it. My only certainty was that it wasn't me. No one demanded payment.

We all, now inebriated, returned to our workplaces and worked.

What that meant was unclear.

***

Spengler's cork popped when Rupert took me out.

Spengler was lonely. Flemish workers only call their mothers for one hour a day if they're lonely. If someone at work does it, check on them. Spengler was far from his mother and homeland and didn't know how to make friends.

Some traders at huge London investment banks don't require pals. Brokers are paid to be your pals. I also existed for Spengler. Spengler was pleased.

Two days after my first meeting with Rupert, Spengler took me to lunch. Snoopy covered the Scandinavian currencies (Spengler's job), and me and Spengler went to have steaks in another cab.

Though I could have used it, Spengler didn't teach me how to eat steaks in the cab. Instead, he described the three brokers and one trader I would meet and their roles in the Swedish Krona Foreign Exchange Swap markets. When we were alone, Spengler only talked about Swedish Foreign Exchange Swap Markets and their participants. There was nothing else I wanted. We would meet:

1. Granty: swarthy, middle-aged, charming, head of Swedish FX swaps broking.
2. Jonesy: bald, significantly older, self-deprecating, shouldn't really be doing this anymore but he's on his third divorce.
3. Bushead: Young, Scouse, Swedish FX broker. Again named for the size and the color of his head.
4. Simon Chang: Young, up-and-coming Swedish FX trader for HSBC. Very smart and has enormous calves. From Hong Kong. Everyone calls him Jet Li, but it's OK because he doesn't mind.

Nobody cared that no one at this meal was Swedish. Within 18 months, I would become a senior Swedish FX exchange dealer without ever visiting Sweden.

The steak restaurant was at the end of several passageways in the City of London, and the dining area was built into the earth. I'm sure the enormous room had electric illumination, but it was so dim and dramatic that I remember it being lit by candles, giving a midday supper a surrealistic and conspiratorial feel.

As we reached the table, I spotted the four men seated together and tried to match their heads to the descriptions. Unbeknownst to Spengler, Bushead, with his red, bulbous head, had been with me and Rupert in Vegas.

After I noticed the brokers, they noticed us too. When they saw Spengler heading to their table, they rose up and cheered, jeered, wailed, clapped, and went wild. I was surprised—Spengler didn't usually get that kind of reception in the office—and I turned to him in confusion to see that the boy was glaring an enormous smile that looked like it could crack his Frankensteinish face and blushing beneath it.

***

From there, the drinking outings multiplied, and I developed an inverse proportionality rule, going out with each trader at a frequency opposite that which I would have chosen if given the choice.

Spengler and Rupert took me out at least once a week (separately, obviously), and their behavior became increasingly terrible in unique ways.

Spengler was worse in the evenings than in the daytime, and his teeth were redder. One young broker from Essex, who couldn't have been over nineteen, kicked him in the backside and shouted, "Take me drinking, Broker Bitch Boy!"

When that happened, the boy wouldn't look back at Spengler, he'd turn and look at me, and he wasn't much younger than I was, and his face had an air of solemn complicity. He wouldn't smile, and I wouldn't smile back at him, so I'd try to meet his stern gaze that burned into my eyes and match his solemnity, and then we'd both nod.

Rupert wanted to take me out in Clapham, Ilford's opposite in London in more than just geography, in the evenings.

It took me hours to get back from there, and sometimes we stayed out so late that I missed the last train and Rupert had to pay for a taxi home, so I didn't like going, but I had to because he wanted me to meet all his friends.

And his friends all had beautiful, monogrammed, freshly ironed shirts and expensive haircuts. My Topman shirts were "non-iron", so they started calling me "Gary the Geezer" and I started sounding more Essex than usual.

One of his pals, Pippy-Holloway, a Goldman Sachs trader, had been with us in Vegas and suffered a nosebleed in the limo. He was always there when we went out. At a fancy-dress house party at Rupert's, I was dressed as Robin and Rupert let me bring Harry from the street, who was dressed as Batman. It was the first time we'd seen anyone take cocaine in person, and Pippy-Holloway introduced me to his girlfriend.

She was beautiful, in a porcelain kind of way, and she was dressed in white like a fairy or something, and I was so shocked to find out that Poppy had a girlfriend after all the things I'd seen him do in Vegas. I looked at her and felt sorry for her, but she seemed happy and smiling, so what could I do? I smiled at her, shook hands, and said, "Hi, I'm Gary, yeah it's lovely to meet you too."

I didn't chat to her for long, but I asked how long she'd been dating Pippy-Holloway, and she said they'd been dating for years.

Rupert and Spengler weren't the only ones targeting me; everyone participated. I could join JB in the pub drinking with the brokers whenever I wanted, and Hong, Snoopy, and sometimes Caleb would join. Snoopy would take me out with his brokers whenever he could, and I was always pleased to go since I felt safe with him and he seemed happy as long as he was eating expensive food. Harry from the street, maybe some other street kids, and brokers would join us every Wednesday to play football and then go out for beers.

My favorite part about hanging out with brokers was seeing them with various traders in different locales. Bushead was Spengler's broker because he broke Skandis, yet he was in Vegas with me, Rupert, and the other euro traders. Jonesy, who was at my lunch with Spengler, was Snoopy's Canadian dollar trader and often went to lunch with him. Bighead, my adoptive city grandfather, had lunch with me and Rupert, but he was Bill's Sterling broker.

This was intriguing because the brokers were always different at the traders' lunches and dinners. I had a different Bushead in Vegas, who insulted celebrities' transportation choices, than in the steak restaurant with Spengler. The Bighead who ate sushi with Rupert was different from the one who drank in riverside taverns with Bill. The brokers were controlled, stoic, and tough about the Deutsche Bank euro trader while working for Rupert. They were aggressive, rude, and nasty with Spengler, talking only about the boy and the market. They discussed rugby with JB. Golf and food were their Snoopy activities. Brokers changed voices and appearances. They seemed to know what each merchant desired. Spengler wanted red wine, white tablecloths, and nightclubs. Rupert wanted pricey sushi and bars. Caleb sought prestigious athletic events when he went out. Billy desired Thames views and pub lunches. Brokers rarely asked traders what they wanted or where they wanted to go. They looked to osmotize. Just knew.

Brokers offered me cocaine. Exactly once. I declined. It was never presented again. It might be on my permanent record. I pondered what else would go there.

3

At the counter, things were shifting as this was happening everywhere. I was on the floor every morning before seven, sitting behind Spengler's shoulder, attempting to understand FX swaps. Though flawed, Spengler was a good teacher and trader who educated me.

Simply put, FX swaps are loans. The loan is collateralized. Example: You give the pawn shop your gold watch and they lend you £200. Another collateralized loan. You borrowed £200 and gave the pawn shop your gold watch as "collateral." "Collateral" is a security you provide the lender that they can keep if you don't pay. That reduces loan risk. One could call this loan a "swap." Lender gave you money, and you gave him your gold watch. You both return it, therefore it's a trade, right? A "cash-for-gold-watch" transaction. In an FX swap, you give foreign currency instead of a gold watch as collateral. The security for a £200 loan is €232 at today's exchange rate. A collateralized loan and a "FX swap" (currency-for-currency swap).

It poses a question. When you borrow money from a pawn store, you pay interest, not the pawnbroker. Who pays interest in an FX swap when you both borrow money—pounds or euros? Simply put, you both do! One pays the interest rate in pounds, which is roughly 4.5%, while the other pays in euros, 3.5%, give or take. They cancel out, and the pound borrower, with the higher interest rate, pays the euro borrower the difference, around 1%.

Who uses these? Basically everyone. FX swaps are ideal for investment funds, hedge funds, and corporations having revenue in one currency and investments in another. That might be The Gap building a Bangladesh sweatshop or your grandfather's pension fund buying Japanese stocks. Each item is a foreign exchange swap. They are one of the world's largest financial products by daily volume.

Got it? Great. I promise it is the best description of an FX swap you will ever get, and it's exactly how Spengler presented it to me, though his was much lengthier and boring.

Since FX swap trading, a trading floor backwater, was becoming profitable, I decided to learn about them.

My desk junior position included collecting the desk PnL, so I understood this. "Profit and Loss," or PnL, is the only thing that matters. I obtained daily PnL estimates from traders at the conclusion of each day.

When I interned in 2007, a successful STIRT trader made $10 million a year. Traders often make $40,000 a day. No trader would make that every day, and every trader would sometimes lose, but a skilled trader would be shooting for that run rate and have the ten million figure as a goal, or "ten bucks," as STIRT traders would say.

Traders make this money for the bank. Not their own money. Trading dealers earn a normal income (my pay at the time was £36,000, which I thought was huge) and a PnL-based "bonus" at the end of the year. How the PnL incentive was calculated was a mystery to me then.

By late summer 2008, daily PnLs began to rise. Traders who were comfortable with $50,000 started making $100,000 or $200,000 once or twice a week. Bill made almost $1 million in late August. It was unparalleled.

My daily PnL calculations were emailed to New York. After each day, the computer systems calculated an accurate daily, monthly, and yearly PnL for each trader and emailed it to everyone. Five traders—Rupert, Billy, JB, Spengler, Hongo—made $10 million by August. Billy, Spengler, and Hongo were over twenty.

Not just STIRT traders saw each other's PnL. Everyone on the floor could see it on an internal website. Every trader on the floor knew that, in the final third of 2008, the bank's top three traders were an old gray Liverpudlian who looked like a hobbit, an Afrikaans imbecile, and the junior euro dealer on the STIRT desk.

STIRT PnLs were exceptionally high when I arrived in June, but most of this money had been produced in July and August, and I didn't understand why. Billy and Caleb were the only ones who understood it structurally, saying "the LIBOR had shot up." That could have been "because Venus is in retrograde" for all I know. The other traders didn't seem to care why it was occurring; all that mattered was that they were finally making the PnL they earned after years of disrespect. It showed in their demeanor and how they were watched as they strolled around the floor. JB was happier as ever and hardly at the desk. Already a trading floor star, Caleb became a legend. Billy started talking too. Rupert, who hadn't made the top three, was the only one who didn't seem to be having fun.

Although pleasantly delighted, no one else seemed startled by this development. They pretended to have a birthday after ten years. Besides, why be surprised? Make hay when the sun shines, I suppose. Making as much hay as possible.

Personally, I would have liked a little hay, but while I now knew what an FX swap was, I didn't understand how all this money was created, and while I wanted to ask Spengler, he was just as interested in generating money as everyone else. Additionally, I had to understand trade coverage.

The days passed that way. I regularly arrived at 6:20 a.m., giving me time with Billy, who was increasingly convinced that the world economy would collapse as August progressed. I should have been scared, but he was laughing and happy and said he would earn a lot of money from it, so I assumed it was a joke.

After everyone got in, I did some admin work on my computer for an hour or two, then sat with Spengler and tried to study cover trade until one of us went on a broker lunch.

To be honest, cover trading was easy. You get called for a price, check where it should be with a couple of brokers, all of whom I knew by now, put the FX swap dates in a little software program made for the desk and it makes some price suggestions, you adjust that price to reflect whether you want to borrow or lend, and then it's done. You then decide whether to keep the deal (because you like it), hedge out quickly for a tiny profit, or negotiate for more money. I soon covered for Caleb, Spengler, and Snoopy when they left the desk.

September included several events. First, the usual grad plan began, bringing in a lot of green-as-you-like students my age to conduct classroom work upstairs on the top floor for their financial examinations. Yes, I had to take my financial exams on the top floor too. The end of the world became more serious.

Each speakerbox had a little button next to and identical to the broker buttons. If you pressed it, you could talk "on the hoot," which blared from every floor speakerbox. It was always funny when a trader came back from a broker lunch four beers too long and tried to yell at the broker he'd just been drinking with, but unintentionally hit the wrong button and wound up on the funny side.

Caleb began holding a morning meeting on the hoot every day to discuss the LIBOR statistic, which I still didn't comprehend, and its effects on the global banking system and economy.

I realized that the collapse of the global banking system was swiftly shifting from "impossibility" to "almost certainly not going to happen," and then to "very, very unlikely," which was not encouraging.

STIRT desk staff seemed unconcerned. Indeed, they appeared content. Because when "LIBOR" rose and the global banking system capitulated, everyone made more money.

The guys on the credit desks—the credit trading desk where I interned the summer before and the credit structuring desk where Matic slept—had sold the world a lot of apparently worthless bullshit for billions of dollars, which would have been fine if they hadn't sold it to our bank as well. That was a major error. They had done it, as had Credit Suisse, Deutsche Bank, and JPMorgan, and now everyone knew every bank would fail.

Nuanced STIRT desk opinion. We considered our employer's role in the collapse of the global banking system and economy a moral failing on our part. The humor is obvious. Naturally, no one considered that. Why did we think that? Despite being pricks, the credit traders sat on the other side of the floor and watched them get fat like pigs in pink shirts. Those men have been making more than us for years, so fuck them, we should get paid.

The traders started making $1 million a day, 2-3 times a week. No one cared about our employer's impending insolvency. We knew we'd be rescued.

Everyone jokes, "What are they gonna do?" "Send the brown-overall guys to run this?"

Then we'd laugh and make lots of money.

Well, except me. I wasn't making any money, and I was trying to figure out how everyone was making so much, but it was hard. When everyone laughed, I laughed too.

And then it occurred.

***

Nobody expected Lehman to fail.

Lehman employed two of my buddies. Remember Sagar Malde? From LSE? Kenyan man. Totally pleasant man. He worked at Lehman. He started the graduate scheme as a dealer. My old Ilford grammar school friend. His name was Jalpesh Patel. He also started at Lehman. He was admitted under an ethnic minority representation program.

They didn't expect Lehman to fail.

Everyone expected Lehman would be bailed out after Bear Stearns, a smaller American investment bank, died like a canary in the coal mine a few months earlier and was bailed out.

Caleb said that every morning on the hoot.

They were not rescued. Jalpesh Patel and Sagar Malde lost their jobs. Having started their careers two weeks earlier, they were handed small "Lehman Brothers" duffel bags to carry.

One part of me felt horrible that they lost their jobs, but another part thought, that's how it goes, right? You should have chosen better banks.

Another part of me asked, "What the fuck are you talking about?" You gained your job in a fucking card game without doing any research, and your bank is under as well, man. If the cards had landed differently, you would be on TV packing your shit into a Citigroup bag.

I'm not sure if I said that or made it up to feel better. I kept thinking, dude, I'm still dancing. There's money to be made, and the music continues.

That strategy had one major flaw: my employer was already insolvent, as everybody with half a brain understood. Even I knew.

When Caleb stated on the hoot that our bank's near-term foreclosure was no longer "very, very unlikely" but rather "we estimate less than a 25% chance," I was strangely more reassured.

But when I went to the top floor to learn about bond mathematics with the other twenty-one-year-olds on the grad program at 9am on Monday, September 15, and told them about the "less than 25 percent chance," they clearly hadn't known. You should have seen their expressions.

Caleb was right—or wrong. Philosophically, that probabilistic forecast is hard to evaluate.

We were rescued. I kept working. That Citibank duffel bag didn't have to hold my crap. What else can be said except to thank God?

None of us did it then.

***

I arrived at 6:10 a.m. on October 1, 2008, the Monday after the bailout. I was 21. Billy was in. Since it was early, it was dark outside when I entered the desk with him. Bill was sitting down, little, in the corner, and I could see the dark sky through the glass behind him. He was already looking in my direction, grinning like a Scouse monkey and nodding madly. All of this was out of character for Bill, but he had made $30 million the week before, and now that the bank won't fail, he'll probably get compensated. That made him pleased. I still believe Bill made over $100 million that week and hid it. I'll explain how Bill made so much money, but for now, know that he was pleased. Liked Billy a lot. That made me happy too.

Caleb arrived before 6:30, which was unusual for him. All the other traders arrived shortly after, considerably earlier than usual. There was barely anyone else on the trade floor, and we were all sitting at our blazing displays in the darkness. It felt like midnight mass.

All was quiet until Billy spun his chair into the aisle and shouted, "So Caleb, what do you think of the bailouts then?"

Caleb stared forward, held his chin with his left hand, and thought for a moment before saying, "I don't know Billy..." It feels like dad bailing you out."

It was the first, last, and only time I heard someone on the trading floor talk about the bailouts ethically.

Everyone returned to their screens and traded, making more money than ever before.

***

So. Why did the STIRT desk profit from Lehman and the bailouts?

Most big banks worldwide, especially in America, went insolvent at that time. For two basic reasons, banks stopped lending to each other:

Not lending to a bankrupt person is wise.

Almost bankrupt? Don't lend money.

These are wise life rules. Note them.

As I mentioned, FX swaps are loans, therefore if nobody makes loans, they're pricey. This loan is collateralized, so if your borrower goes

44

bankrupt, you don't lose a lot. When the world is on the brink of bankruptcy, these are the only loans you can make.

We were the only ones playing.

We observed all spreads explode. Remember trading spreads? 67–69? I-buy-at-67-and-I-sell-at-69? Imagine if it becomes 47–89 and you have regular traders on both sides. Where you used to play with 2's, one buyer and seller guarantees a 42 profit. Eat as much as you can at the buffet.

They dined. No one ate more than Spengler.

Spengler was always evil. He loved ripping customers and making money. He was a true trader. In July, he'd ripped a customer so hard that the salesperson had come back and complained to Caleb. Caleb asked Spengler what he was doing, and Spengler, who was seated, looked up at him with his arms spread out and said, "It's not my fault Caleb, it's my job!"

Caleb saw Spengler like a father sees his son, put his arm around his shoulder, leaned into him, and said, "It's not your job to rip the customers Spengler. You must tear and make them smile."

That was always remembered. It seems Spengler forgot it sometimes. He frequently forgot it after Lehman.

Spengler made two million dollars ripping a customer that week after the bailout. Two million bucks in one trade.

After that, he was so excited that he rushed out of his swivel chair and into the aisle, taking a deep lunge that must have made his cream chinos see their whole existence flash before their eyes. His massive head bounced with his large mouth gaping and his arms were fist-pumping, and the sight was so monstrous that everyone turned their chairs around.

Caleb leaped from his chair and grabbed the child like a football steward takes and wraps a streaker. He held him by the shoulders and pressing into him, their noses almost touching, and he whispered, "What the fuck are you doing?" What the hell are you doing?

As he repeated it, Spengler arched his head backward and his mouth trembled, trying to form words but failing. All he could say was, "B–b–but—I—b–b–b–but I—"

"Shut the fuck up," Caleb said, pointing across the trading floor and telling Spengler, "Look over that way. Look over there. See those guys? Their fucking jobs end this week. Do you grasp that? You're standing here fist-pumping like a crazy as they lose their jobs this week. You're doing what, Spengler? Want to be paid here? Yeah? Do you want money?

Remember that query. Want to get paid?

***

A huge problem arose throughout. It may have caught your eye.

Due to large spreads, STIRT traders are profiting. Who profits from wide spreads? Books belong to the owners. Spengler made all the Skandi spread money and JB made all the yen spreads since he traded them. Rupert made all the euros, and Bill made pounds.

I traded for what? Nothing. How much did I make? Jack crap.

That's the issue.

We need a fresh plan.

What if I can't access the books' money to generate money when everyone else is?

Bill made the most money.

Billy was doing what?

Bill did this, it turns out.

Bill has long doubted the global economy. He saw rising global indebtedness and didn't think you could run an economy by lending to dickheads. He expected the math-genius-credit-traders' stuff to blow up because he suspected them to be spoiled rich idiots.

He was premature and had been betting on this explosion for years. This likely lost him a few million dollars in PnL in each of the preceding three years, explaining why Citibank had not been successful and why Rupert believed he was an idiot.

Billy wasn't stupid.

Billy was banking on interest rate divergence. Imagine borrowing money for three months. You do what? You ask your bank, mother, mafia, or whoever you get loans from for a three-month loan, right? Simple. There's another option for large banks, investment funds, and corporations. If you're a large institution, you can call Citibank for a one-day loan. I need money for three months, not one day, so that doesn't help. Actually, that's fine. After the loan matures tomorrow, you borrow money from another big lender, possibly Deutsche Bank, for a day. You have two days. You'll giggle after three months of doing that daily. If you wish to borrow money for three months, you can take one loan or ninety loans for one day.

Which do you pick? Which do you prefer? You may be thinking, I'd rather take three months to figure it out and know the interest rate. However, foreign money markets may readily arrange 90 single-day loans in advance, so you can fix interest rates in both circumstances.

The right answer is that borrowers prefer 90-day loans and lenders prefer single-day loans. If you lend someone money for ninety days and they go bankrupt on day twenty-five, you're screwed, but if you lent them money for one day, you're not. If you borrow money for one day and people realize you're going bankrupt on day twenty-five, you're screwed, but if you borrowed for ninety days, you might have a chance.

This didn't matter before 2008 because banks didn't fail. That changed in 2008. Ninety-day loans disappeared, whereas one-day lending remained stable. Little gray Billy seemed to be the only City resident who saw that coming. He bet on it for years. He made tens of millions in a week and more after that. Turns out his prediction that the world economy will explode was accurate. After years of ridicule, he was right. He fucking loved it.

Would you?

That didn't fix my issue. Since that bet was gone. Two weeks ago, I should have made it. Once a trader makes $40 million, it's probably too late.

So I did what? Returned to Spengler.

Spengler was the only other trader on the desk making too much money besides Bill.

Hongo, like Bill, made over $100 million that year, making him the desk's second most lucrative trader. However, Hongo was on the euro book and Spengler traded Skandis. Books with the highest profit were listed on the desk, and Skandis were near the bottom.

How did Spengler make so much? If I could get him to show me, I could make some.

The rapid aftermath of Lehman left little time for thought. Nobody wanted to undertake cover trading because they were earning so much money on their own books, and Caleb was always off the desk meeting with bigwigs to make sure everyone got paid. So I covered most of the time.

In November, markets calmed and Caleb returned to work. That got me back behind Spengler, who had already made a lot. Though young, he was sure he would be one of the bank's top traders that year, and it was getting to him. For me, that was fine. When Spengler was too large for his boots, he only wanted to talk about trading and himself. We shared identical interests.

He showed me a huge spreadsheet he used to make so much money when I inquired how. A masterpiece. It divided the Swedish "Stokkie" FX swap market into days. Stokkie borrowing on December 14 costs how much? What about May 23? Spengler analyzed every day and compared the market price to his ideal price. He gave me a spreadsheet I used for years.

Spengler detailed his "position," or list of trades, as we looked through the spreadsheet. In the Stokkie FX exchange market, that indicated how much Swedish krona he borrowed or lent daily. He always had a mysterious purpose for each exchange.

One thing stood out as we examined Spengler's perspective. He borrowed Swedish krona daily. FX swaps are loans, right? It's a swap, thus it's a two-way loan. Besides borrowing, you lend. Spengler lent US cash for his Swedish krona book. The situation seemed odd. You might have assumed he borrowed Swedish krona on cheap days and lent it on pricey days. Instead, he borrowed Swedish krona and lent US dollars against it every day for two years. The only difference was his loan amount.

He did that, why?

I checked the other traders' FX swap books later that afternoon. Every day, Billy lent US dollars. So was Snoopy, but smaller. Caleb and JB did it too. They loaned money daily for two years.

Before nightfall, I asked Spengler.

"Why are people lending money? Why no dollar borrowing?

Spengler looked at me like a fool.

Why the hell would we borrow US dollars? Borrowing US currency is stupid."

I tried to look non-retarded in my face. It must have failed since Spengler sighed and opened his spreadsheet.

"What's the dollar interest rate now? One percent, right? It drops to 0%. But look at the FX swap interest rate." He played with some numbers in the sheet's corner. We receive over 3%. Free money."

I didn't require repeated confirmation. I was thinking about how to ask for some of the exchange while he was talking. While pondering what to respond, I quickly noticed he was looking at me and asking, "So?" You want some?

What do you think?

***

Let's open up and make sure you're still with me.

FX swaps are loans. Each party borrows one currency from the other. They both pay interest, so only one pays the interest differential. If pounds are 3% and dollars are 2%, the pound borrower pays 1%.

Individual currency interest rates—who sets them?

There's a gorgeous old structure in your capital city, or Frankfurt if you're European, called the "Central Bank." The Bank of England or Bank of Japan—your home bank—will likely be its name. US Federal Reserve or Fed. The ECB is in Europe. In that expensive edifice, affluent mummy's boys who never graduated strive every year and fail to save your economy. They eat a lavish meal in a wood-paneled hall.

Though you may not realize it, these people are crucial to your life and this story.

Now, all you need to know about these individuals is that they set interest rates for every country, including yours. (Bill had his own cab driver who drove him home from broker dinners to his Hertfordshire property whenever he missed the last train. I had a drink with that driver, Sid, and he told me that whenever Bill was really drunk, he would make Sid stop outside the Bank of England so he could go into an alley around the back and piss on the Bank. Sid stated that Bill would insist on that, even if it was not on the way home. Respected that greatly.

In late 2008, central banks throughout the world aggressively cut interest rates to zero in the belief that it would revitalize national economies. This happened to practically every currency on the desk: pound, euro, Swiss franc, Swedish and Danish krone, American and Canadian dollars. When you include the Japanese yen, which had zero interest rates for nearly twenty years, almost all major currencies would soon reach zero.

How does that affect FX swaps? If the payout on an FX swap equals the interest rate differential and practically all interest rates are moving to zero, then the differentials must also be zero, right? All FX swaps should be free then!

However, Spengler informed me that FX swaps were not free. Free one-day FX swaps were virtually nil. But borrowing US cash for more than a few weeks or a month was quite expensive. This gave FX swap traders a great opportunity to lend dollars for three months and borrow them back daily. Spengler said it was free money.

Real free money never exists. Is it? Could making money be so easy? If it was easy, why wasn't everyone doing it? Actually, everyone did it. Was it free? The risks?

As I sat behind Spengler watching him swing his huge spreadsheet, I could have asked myself these questions. I didn't ask. I nodded and replied, "Yeah man, for sure, I want some."

Spengler pressed the button, spoke to Granty, and put the trade on for me. I lent $240 million in a dollar/Stokke FX swap with Danske Bank Copenhagen for three months. I went home that day happy, and it was my first medium-sized trade.

Once home, eating supper with my parents and watching a tiny fuzzy black-and-white TV with a dial, I thought, "Wait a minute, what the fuck am I doing?" Foreign exchange swaps between dollars and Stokkies are unfamiliar to me. I've never visited Sweden. What the hell do I know that Danske Bank Copenhagen doesn't? Isn't $240 million a bit much?

The STIRT desk often traded in billions and called them "yards," so two hundred and forty million dollars was not a big trade to them. However, that was a lot of money, and talking about a trade is very different from doing one. I barely slept that night.

I arrived early the next day. Must chat to Bill.

Billy was shocked that I was waiting for him that morning. All the questions I should have asked the day before finally came to mind. Putting your money, reputation, and job at risk for an opinion will make you question its validity. That should be considered while watching the news.

Billy was looking at me suspiciously when he came in and spotted me seated next to his chair. I told him what I did before he sat.

"I lent $240 million to a three-month Stokkie."

Bill laughed immediately. He found that hilarious.

Fuckin hell, did you? Finally grew balls and lent cash, yeah? Hey Gal, why did you do that?

The man was pissed.

No sugar coating.

«Spengler said it was free money»

He stared at me like an idiot when I revealed the truth. To defend myself, I said, "Everyone does it." I checked everyone's position. Everybody does it. You're doing it!"

Billy grinned and nodded, changing his mood. He definitely would have ruffled my hair if I hadn't shaved it off, but I had, so he touched my nose. He turned away and checked his screens.

You fucking cockney twat, not as dumb as you look. Are we all doing it? I see you're doing it too." He laughed, turned on his nine monitors, and took his Financial Times from his backpack.

"Why are they all doing it? What's at risk?

After dropping his Financial Times, Bill stared at me with earnestness. "Well, well, well, well," Billy said, fucking loving it. Someone really grew a pair overnight, right? "What are the risks?"

"No idea. Spengler claimed free money. Perhaps there are no risks."

"Good fucking answer, why did you do it if you don't know the risks?"

"I did it because you did, Bill."

That made Bill smile. "Great response again. Why? I'll explain. This is because the globe wants US dollars, and Citibank is the biggest American bank in the world. We have the dollars, and they don't, so we'll charge them whatever we want and get paid. OK? Do you comprehend?

I nodded.

"Now I'll tell you something even more important, right? Never say there's a risk-free trade in your life. OK? Credit cunts thought that, and looked at what happened to them. You'll fuck off and sit in your corner after I say one final thing, the most crucial thing. One circumstance will blow up this transaction and cost us all our fuckin arses. If the global banking system crashes, trade will explode. This place sinks if it happens. You and I will lose our jobs, bringing down the world economy. We gambled against it. Will we be right? We'll get paid. After that, we'll all have a few drinks, and you will too. You should probably go back to your seat and think about what that implies. You make it the last time you undertake a trade without knowing the hazards. It's a good fucking trade, Gal. You did well."

He was already back in his screens, and I was back in my seat. It wasn't the last time I conducted a deal without knowing the risks, which may have saved me a lot of problems over the years. However, as Bill and

Spengler told me, it was a good fucking trade, and by Christmas I had made 700 grand.

***

It's hard to believe how much fun it was to go out drinking, eating raw chicken, learning about trading, covering traders while they were drunk, and making my first 700 grand PnL in those first few months on the desk. It seemed like days and nights blurred into one. JB was always there with a joke and a smile, and Caleb noticed my good work. And even if Rupert was dangerous and Spengler disgusting, it didn't matter because everyone was making money.

Although I wasn't making much money at the time, I could sense it coming. The PnL was coming, and my thirty-six grand paycheck was more than I'd ever had. I went to restaurants for the first time and made transactions on the trading floor in sharp shoes and a Bluetooth earpiece. Would you want more?

It seemed like a family for the first time in a long time, beyond all else. Billy and Caleb were like two different fathers, one short and scrappy and sweary and the other massive and impossibly smooth, Rupert and JB were the mean and friendly uncles at Christmas, and Snoopy and Spengler were my big brothers.

On the rare nights I went home to have dinner with my real folks, they harassed me for rent and car repairs. I had to give them the car money, but I told my mum I was paying my dad's rent and my dad that I was giving it to my mum, and neither of them understood that for ages, and everything felt like it was coming together.

***

The big one followed. I think it was my first huge trading shock.

It was unexpected. You know Caleb was only 29. At seven thirty one morning, the busiest time of the day, he marched the entire crew off the desk and toward one of the corner offices. I thought someone had died.

In the back corner next to Bill, Caleb was leading the long line of traders off the floor, so when I gulped down my coffee and took off my headset to chase them, JB, not Caleb, turned around and shouted, "Not you Gary, someone's got to stay on the desk."

I stood and stared, thinking, "What the fuck?"

Snoopy's speakerbox started beeping, then Hongo's, then Spengler's, then Bill's, and I was running and spinning between them, making prices in euros, yen, krona, and pounds, flicking up the little switches to everybody's brokers, all of whom I knew by now, and making all the prices. I felt like Roy Keane or Steven Gerrard, marshalling the whole thing from the middle.

Then I thought, "Damn, I can do this alone, maybe I don't need the rest." Maybe just me, Snoopy, and Bill…"

I was so engrossed in this wild dance that I didn't notice that all the traders had marched back to the counter, and Billy hit me so hard in the shoulder that my Bluetooth headset fell off and he shouted, "Caleb's gone and fucking quit!!!"

***

Caleb was leaving, retiring at twenty-nine, married, and a father, and decided to construct a large fucking mansion in California and live his life there with his family. Probably good for him.

How did it affect me?

My initial thought was worry.

Caleb hired me. Caleb was my main sponsor. Caleb promised me I could trade right away. Still 22, I was. It was unusual for a man my age and experience to have a PnL and conduct his own trading. What if the new boss broke the deal?

Who would be the next boss? Would it be a desk employee? Is someone outside brought in? Billy, the bank's most lucrative trader the year before, would undoubtedly be offered the job, but we all knew he wouldn't accept. Billy merely wanted to trade and publicly hated the bigwigs. Getting promoted would entail more politics and less trading. Billy would never accept it. Snoopy believed they would give it to a terrible frog-like New York Slug trader if Billy didn't take it.

However, Caleb's departure was not the only news. At twenty-nine, Caleb left to build his own house in Northern California and never work again. This guy made how much? I knew the desk had made a lot of money last year, maybe half a billion dollars, but I didn't know how. Even departing at 29—retiring. That mean?

***

I had two goodbye dinners with Caleb. One was a lavish supper with the whole desk in the early May sunshine at the same Spanish restaurant by the water where Rupert and I had eaten the pig.

The changing weather was lovely. The sun was shining again, evenings were rising later and the mood was festive. Everyone congratulated Caleb. Caleb lived his dream.

All floor traders talk about quitting. They say, "I'll go next year after my bonus. They don't deserve me; I'll go next year.

Nobody leaves until pushed.

Traders fantasize about a mountain or seaside home and a rural family. Younger, possibly single, people talk about cycling to India and sailing to Chile.

Nobody goes.

Caleb was leaving. Still youthful and gorgeous at 29. Nothing gray had appeared on his head yet. Great hero. He was doing what everyone wanted and hadn't offended anyone. Anyway, no one I liked.

We all sat around this long rectangular table with endless plates of cheese, chorizo, olives, and other things I didn't understand. I didn't like that kind of food and would have rather had a proper dinner, but I was glad to be with everyone, laughing, eating, and joking as the high sun sank into the river. I was just glad there was no baby pig.

Billy questioned Caleb, "What about your deferred stock?"

I didn't understand the query, but Caleb's smile, known from the Trading Game, attracted my attention. He replied, "Don't worry, I took care of it."

"Charity?"

"Charity."

"But the Slug?"

"One year without bonus."

"He took that?"

55

"He did."

The other traders weren't listening, but I kept looking at Caleb, who was nodding deeply and smiling, and Billy, who appeared more serious but was nodding, and even though I didn't understand what they were saying, I recalled it. My doing so was crucial.

After everyone was inebriated and the sun was almost set, JB asked Caleb, "Do you have any regrets?"

After contemplating the sunset, Caleb added, "Only one, that we couldn't fuck Rupert. Do not worry. Be patient. We will."

We laughed, raised glasses and drank beer late at night.

***

Caleb and I had another goodbye supper. It was a farewell lunch.

Caleb approached me after his desk announcement. I understood why I couldn't be in the meeting when he told everyone, and he apologized for leaving so soon after hiring me and making promises he couldn't make. He promised to look after me, take me out for lunch anywhere I wanted, and answer any question honestly.

Ask him to take me to Chili's. They make good buffalo wings. With blue cheese dip. We went.

We started early on the STIRT desk and ate lunch early, so when we got to Chili's, a massive, well-lit fast-food restaurant high up in the Canary Wharf retail center, it was still vacant and not even lunchtime. Just got my buffalo wings.

We were sad sitting in that vast, open restaurant alone. Twenty-four buffalo wings and two little pots of blue cheese dip separated us on a small, square plastic table. Seven years separated us, but sitting across from me and twice my stature, he would have looked like my dad to a stranger.

I regarded him. That black helmet of thick dark hair frames a huge head. He looked drained. He appeared happy. He appeared completed. I had known him for 2.5 years. I expected to miss him. It resembled the last day of primary school. You miss your friends and teacher, but you don't know what to say.

Naturally, I didn't inform him.

I stared at him and asked, "So," "I have one question?"

That's right."

He was smiling heartily and squinting slightly from the bright sun streaming through a skylight and throwing sharp beams on our table.

"And you'll answer honestly?"

I will, Gazza."

Large, wide smile.

Want to ask anything?

Question of your choice."

I dropped my wing.

"What do I do to get paid 100,000 pounds?"

Caleb laughed loudly and fell backward, dropping his bone-bone wing.

"A hundred thousand pounds? Bonus??"

Hundred thousand pounds. Bonus."

He paused, staring at me incredulously.

"It's impossible. You cannot make that in your first year."

I didn't laugh when Caleb laughed again. Held his eyes. Twenty-two was my age. I attempted to look manly.

Caleb stopped laughing.

Tell me what to do, and I will."

He was seeing I was serious, yet he kept answering the same.

A 100,000-pound incentive is impossible in your first year as a trader. Not possible. You cannot."

Tell me what to do, and I will."

It was long before Caleb spoke. His hand was on his chin as he studied me.

You must earn $10 million for the bank.

In the afternoon, I opened the printer next to the desk and took two blank white A4 sheets.

On my first paper, I wrote "12 MILLION DOLLARS," in uppercase. Extra two million dollars was an error margin. Under that, I wrote five trades with calculated annual profits of $12 million each. The trades:

1. Lend one billion dollars one year Swissy FX Swap

2. Lend one billion dollars one year Yen FX Swap
3. Lend 1.3 billion dollars one year Sterling FX Swap
4. Lend 1.5 billion dollars one year Canada FX Swap
5. Lending $1.4 billion a year Stokkie FX Swap.

I folded the piece of paper and I put it in my desk drawer.

I wrote the exact same thing on the second piece of paper, folded that one up, put it in the back pocket of my trousers, took it home, and kept it in my underwear drawer which was under my bed.

They were big trades and I was too junior to execute them. Plus, they weren't my currencies. They were other people's books.

How could I get one of them?

**

Late May was Caleb's last day. He had removed all his belongings from the desk the week before, so he just had to shake our hands. He left his job two hours early in the afternoon. It was around 3 p.m.

JB exclaimed, "Caleb Zucman is leaving the building!" as he left the desk and went down the aisle.

After we stood up and clapped, everyone on the floor did too.

I saw the gigantic man's back walk down the aisle alone. The first trader I knew. He didn't turn, raise a hand, or acknowledge the cheers. He left without looking back.

**

We all wanted to know the new boss. We knew Bill would decline. We feared it might be the New York Frog. Chuck, not the Frog. Mathieson was huge.

I've generously depicted traders as huge throughout this book because most were far larger than me. Huge Chuck was the biggest.

Chuck was Canadian. I'd never traveled to Canada. He was probably from Toronto or Vancouver, but when I saw him, I imagined him as a lumberjack in a freezing, snowy wilderness lugging massive trees home on his back. His height was around six feet seven. He appeared as a giant, not a fat man, despite his beautifully bulging tummy. An honest goliath. Belying his stature was a kind visage that kept him from being intimidating, but I only noticed it from below. He

58

resembled a giant version of my father in his early forties, square-jawed and with a crisp salt-and-pepper side parting. His gigantism and amiability captivated me and wanted to know more.

Trading floor legend Chuck. Trading the Russian rouble. You know the STIRT desk traded primarily "rich-world," "Western" currencies. Where trains ran on time. Despite being near our desk, the "Emerging market" desks traded Russia, India, and Brazil's currencies. Chuck traded roubles before I was born. He was reportedly acquainted with Putin.

Chuck was well-known and large, but none of us on the STIRT desk knew him. When he rose up and strolled around the trade floor, his vertiginous head bounced over the screen-walls so everyone could see where he was. In the weeks after Caleb left, rumors spread that he would be the next boss. I confirmed the rumor this way.

After Caleb left, there was no Swiss franc trader or desk head until a new one was hired. Therefore, Bill was temporary manager and I was temporary Swiss franc dealer. The trades went into mine, not Caleb's book, which no longer existed. Back then, the Swiss currency book was profitable, and I was making good money.

Bill despised managing and admin, and as his junior, I handled a lot of admin. I often had to stay after everyone went home, but I didn't mind because I was making money.

I was alone on the desk for a late afternoon two or three weeks into this period, performing tedious admin, sending emails, and booking trades. Chuck, who had not yet been named STIRT desk head, came over to me.

Looking up at Chuck. With me reclining and him standing, our faces were far apart. Chuck had to tilt his neck forward like he was gazing at his shoes to look at me. He shone. I grinned.

I shook Chuck's hand. He knew my name.

"Hi Gary, Chuck."

He then went for a chair. There were vacant chairs everywhere because all the other STIRT dealers had gone home, so this should not have been a protocol. But he left for two minutes. Maybe he needed a stronger chair.

Chuck reappeared and slowly rolled the chair next to me and sank into it. The man's massive bulk and weight gave his motions enormous gravity. I felt really boylike.

After getting into the chair, Chuck smiled mischievously at me without saying anything.

I smiled awkwardly and continued booking transactions since I didn't know what to do.

After two absurd minutes, Chuck leaned forward and said, "Hey."

I turned to him and asked, "Hey?" He was still smiling like a mad schoolboy.

Chuck brought his right hand around, which I hadn't known he'd been hiding behind his back. The hand held a copy of Sports Illustrated, a swimsuit magazine.

After looking at the magazine cover, I gazed at Chuck's face. He wiggled his eyebrows at me.

Magazine opened by Chuck. Not to read it himself, but to indicate that we were to look at the photographs together. A bikini-clad woman was shown on two pages.

After viewing the photo, I looked at Chuck. He kept wiggling eyebrows. He wiggled them more and replied, "Yes." You like that? Of course, I said "Yes." It's nice.

Chuck turned the page.

The next page had another bikini-clad double-page spread. Chuck responded, "Mmmm, yeah." I saw his wiggling eyebrows. Very nice."

I answered, "Yeah, that's nice."

And I nodded.

This continued for too long to explain. At some point, maybe after the third or fourth bikini, I recognized that Chuck was the new desk head. There was no other explanation. As we read the magazine, the feeling solidified.

Chuck rolled up the magazine and put it in his large trouser pocket once we finished with the bikinis. He stopped smiling and stared into the distance as if he could finally go to work after introductions.

"So, what do you do on the desk?"

I stared Chuck in the eye, and Chuck looked youthful.

It was unfathomable that Chuck, who would take over the STIRT desk in a week, didn't know my job. Was it? Was it?

I stared him in the eye and attempted to gauge him. Why was he here? Was this a lie?

I thought the new boss would be the Swiss franc trader and I would be the modest Kiwi trader and cover for Bill as Caleb had filled that role. Chuck surely understood my role. Or did he?

I watched him. Was it a game? Was he clueless? Trying to interpret his face. Eventually, he smiled again, so I probably stared too long. As he grinned at me, I smiled back and replied, "I'm the Swiss franc trader, Chuck." I trade Swiss francs."

Chuck grinned and nodded deeply as he gently raised himself out of his reinforced chair, looking up at me occasionally. As he left, he turned to me one last time and remarked, "It was really nice to meet you Gary." Looking forward to working with you."

After Chuck went, I sat alone on the desk and contemplated what had transpired.

I then switched to Morley, my favorite Swiss broker, and shouted, "Morley!" Morley! Still there?

I lowered the switch, and Morley's cockney voice sang, "You alright, Gal?" Why are you still here?

"No worries, mate—can you get me a one-year? Want to lend US dollars."

Mate, everyone's gone home, but I might get you some from New York. Want to do how much?

"I wanna do about a yard".

A yard costs billions.

And I did it. I traded Swiss francs. I traded number one from my sheet. It earned me almost $12 million by year's end.

Yes, I wrote that on the sheet.

4

Nobody had ever made $10 million in their first year. They told me afterward.

So, why was I first?

It may have been my brains or bravery.

Nobody has the nerve to make such significant trades at such a young age.

However, those weren't the key reasons, but they may have contributed. I made a lot of money that year because it was easy and allowed.

It was simple since everyone did it. That deal was repeated by all. Lending cash at 2% for long-term and borrowing them back daily for free.

It was probably approved for the same reason. Because my peers were doing it on a larger scale. Bill was the bank's most lucrative trader again in 2009, making $100 million. No one made 100 million, but a couple made 75. Who cared about me? Sitting in my corner, barely making $12 million. No one cared. Heck, Snoopy made 30 that year. Chuck often lumbered over to me like a pine tree and put a massive shadow on my screens. On those occasions, he didn't speak. He'd smile like the mad or enlightened and rock my chair while gazing aside. He may still be unaware of my employment.

However, the bigger question is how did we all do it? Why did we all make so much money on massive trades? What if we all made the same deal and it went tragically wrong?

I didn't ask Billy until midway through 2009, but he told me that at the start of the crisis, Caleb had gone to the big bosses—not just the Slug, but his boss and his boss's boss—and gotten special permission for us to do the same trade. Billy said we would all profit if the trade produced money—Billy, me, Chuck, the Slug, the Slug's boss, and up.

Even our CEO got PnL pay. If it failed, the banking system would collapse and we'd lose our jobs, so who cared? Therefore, it was allowed. I suppose fish decay from the head down.

I glanced at Chuck and wondered if what he and we were doing was wrong. As usual, Chuck smiled and nodded at nobody. He had just dumped a huge mound of loose change from his drawer onto his desk. He piled coins after counting them.

PART THREE
THERMOSTAT

1

HOW COME PEOPLE WERE NOT Spending? In 2009, 2010, 2011? Titzy called it a confidence crisis. 2008 shook the system. A consumer was severely shaken. After two years, trust is returning in 2011, and people are ready to spend again.

An opinion, I suppose.

What did Bill think?

The banking system sucked. Many were fucked. People lost houses and employment. However, new owners are buying those homes, unemployment is falling, and inflation is rising. After the banking system is fixed, the economy and interest rates will recover.

An opinion, I suppose.

Seven years later, in 2018, I asked affluent, snakeskin-belted Oxford macroeconomics professor Antonio Mancini what he thought. "We knew zero rates would last! Consumption-savings preferences were shaken!"

Well... An opinion, I suppose.

JB has a phrase regarding opinions. "Opinions are arseholes. Everyone has one."

I questioned Harry Sambhi. Harry was young. Harry jumped over tube barriers to save money and had holes in his shoes. He didn't spend it because of that. I questioned Asad. Asad slept on the sofa to pay for a deposit after his mother sold the family house to support him and his sisters. Therefore, they didn't spend. I questioned Aidan. Aidan's mother lost her job and couldn't acquire a new mortgage rate. Aidan had to pay the sky-high monthly charges. Therefore, they didn't spend. Losing their houses. Not even noticed.

I suppose opinions are arseholes. Everyone's got one.

***

Soon after, Citibank rents a vast estate outside London and invites all worldwide traders for a conference and piss-up. I see why they call him the Slug. I see why he's called the Frog.

The Slug's boss gives a big speech telling us to take more risks.

Why not risk ten million dollars if you're willing to risk one million? We all get army camo baseball caps with "Go Big or Go Home" on the front.

I left the celebration. I went into my Peugeot 106 with the cap on and drove home.

As instructed by the Big Boss Man, everyone placed big bets on the desk. Big recovery bets. Billy, Snoopy, JB, Chuck were in. Fuck, Hongo joined despite never betting. Everyone did it—not just the STIRT desk. Spot, Options, Emerging Markets desks. But I waited. I disliked the fragrance. Titzy wasn't in because I wasn't.

I had a meeting the next week. The floor's desk heads met biweekly. I carried sandwiches to every meeting when Caleb was boss. When Chuck arrived, I didn't tell him about the rendezvous and kept going. Unsure why, I felt it might be handy down the road.

One of the bank's few economists I liked led that week's meeting. I recognized him from my internship in credit. He was Timothy Prince. Timothy has many charts. He examined them individually. One country's fiscal status was on each. Italy, Spain, Greece. Portugal, Ireland. Also UK, US, Japan.

Different versions of the same story. Every year, these governments spent more than they earned and accumulated debt. Continuing in the same direction would raise their debt interest rates. Lenders would stop lending, forcing them to sell. Bad idea.

I took all the leftover sandwiches to the desk in a brown paper bag.

I couldn't forget it. I wasn't worried about western welfare state. I couldn't shake this similarity. Same thing. Spanish, American, Japanese governments. The circumstance resembled Asad and Aidan's mothers. Outgoings exceed income. Losing borrowing power.

Increasing debt service income. Asset loss. Same problem. The globe has holes in its shoes, not just Harry.

It ran into Titzy's economics and wisdom. Our system is monetary. Everything must be balanced. Someone has credit for every debtor. Someone gains for every loser. Balance is built into the system. Additionally, what about the houses? What about the increasing stock market? These assets remained. If we, the people, and the governments don't own them... Who did?

I guess it hit me then, surrounded by millionaires and sandwiches.

I looked left. Pink shirt, white, sky blue. I regarded my right. White shirt, pink, pinstripes—rare today. The collar had four letters embroidered in string: "A.I.E.Q." Whose surname starts with Q?

Millionaires. Every single one.

Me too. What about me? My rich status would soon arrive.

It was us. It was us, right? We were balanced. In a world of destitute children, we were the richer lads than our fathers. We balanced Italian debt by expanding bank balances. We received Aidan's mother's mortgage interest, which he now had to pay. And our kids. Maybe my kids. If Asad's mother sold the house, they might own it. Maybe our children might lend that house's rent and Italian government interest to Asad's children, and then we'd own the houses and the loan. It would grow via compound interest. We would buy more assets with asset proceeds. You'd sell us your assets to pay your mortgage and rent. To repay us. It would go like that. Worse would come. It would develop uncontrollably. Not a confidence crisis. Not the banking system fucking. Not an "exogenous shock to consumption savings preferences." It was unfair. This inequality would worsen until it controlled and wrecked the economy. Not transient, but terminal. It ended the economy. It was cancer.

I understood.

I had to acquire green Eurodollars.

European green dollars are bets. A safe bet on American interest rates in 2.5 years. Nothing like FX swaps' convoluted "lend one currency borrow another" nonsense. No more daily loans. This is simply betting. Casino things. Loved it. Billy, Snoopy, and I enjoyed it.

Betting was not our job. Customers were meant to get FX swaps. We received Eurodollars (and their equivalents in all other currencies) to "hedge our risks." We hedged too many risks, frequently without them. About to steal my life's hedge.

That's when I learned why we were all incorrect. We diagnosed terminal cancer as seasonal colds. It seems the financial system was flawed but fixable. We believed confidence would return from its low point. But what was really happening was that the middle class—ordinary, industrious families like Aidan and Asad's and practically all the world's largest governments—was losing wealth to the wealthiest. Normal households lost assets and went into debt. So were governments. As impoverished people and governments got poorer and the wealthiest got richer, interest, rent, and profit from the middle class to the rich increased, aggravating the problem. It would not fix itself. It would worsen and escalate. Few economists consider wealth distribution in their models, thus they didn't notice this. They memorize "representative agent" models for 10 years, which view the economy as one "average" or "representative" person. Thus, for them, the economy is always aggregated and averaged. They disregard dispersion. They consider it a side note. Moralistic facade. Ultimately, my degree proved valuable. It proved everyone incorrect.

If I was right, this mattered. It suggested markets were badly mispriced. There would be no recovery or interest rate normalization. In early 2011, markets were pricing roughly 6 complete US Federal Reserve rises of 0.25% apiece in the following year. They'd be wrong. All would be incorrect. Those rate rises were out. They never happened. I could profit from this year after year when interest estimates were delayed. These fools ignored inequality. At least a decade passed before they understood.

Alternatives to green Eurodollars existed. Could bet with "OIS." Eurodollars were machine-traded and required adjustment, but with an OIS, you could get another bank to offer you a price for a big trade and execute it in one drop. Also, who broke US dollar OIS? Yes, Harry Sambhi. I wanted Harry to see.

Pressed Harry's button. My first trade with Harry. I asked him for a price on $700 million of one-year OIS commencing in spring 2012. I wasn't a dollar trader, so that was a major trade. Shocked, Harry. He may have assumed I was helping. He found a Deutsche Bank price and I hit it. It felt nice. Every fool on the desk was betting on recovery, but I was betting against them. Find out who's right. Everyone, or me. I liked that. Play with the big boys. Game on.

The earthquake followed.

***

How would you feel if an earthquake killed 20,000 people and you made $11 million?

Five hundred fifty bucks each person.

I didn't know about the earthquake. I'm no magician.

I found hundreds of emails at my desk. They included a Citi Macroeconomics employee. It said: "We anticipate the earthquake to be strongly positive for 2011 Japanese GDP growth."

I opened my desk and quietly snapped a blue ballpoint pen in two, dropping both halves into the bin. I repeated with my second pen. Then I got extra pens from the stationery cabinet.

The Tokyo desk junior gave Titzy a video of our Tokyo STIRT trader, Hisa Watanabe, on the trading floor following the earthquake. He was huddled behind his desk, grasping something, but his little head kept coming up in a yellow hard hat and he was attempting to grab his mouse and trade while Tokyo rocked through the windows.

Titzy sent the video to the desk, but no one laughed. You know why they didn't laugh? Earthquakes lower interest rates.

It's odd, right? You study economics for three years and trade it for three. You check 100 emails at 5 a.m. Everyday. You hire a recent college graduate to talk about economic theory all day. Your magnificent idea is finally conceived and bet on. You make 2.5 million dollars in a day, an earthquake kills 20,000 people, and all of your closest friends, the people you spend every day with, the people who taught you to trade, and the people who taught you everything, are destroyed.

It means what?

Titzy continued gazing at me like I was a genius for predicting the earthquake. As if I did anything.

Naturally, Billy, the biggest, lost the most. He probably lost $5–6 million. It was his to lose. Snoogy lost 1.5–2. That was much for him. Pretty basically his year-long PnL. JB attempted to fight it but lost about 4. He fell into the red. Hongo quit instantly and lost $500K. Chuck is like a Teflon Buddha, losing little. How did he do it? Sometimes I doubt he existed. I remained silent. Pens broke while waiting.

A nuclear tragedy occurred. You probably know. People worried the nuclear plant might explode, therefore 154,000 Fukushima residents were evacuated. That boosted my standing. Up $3.5 million. Up $4.5 million.

Within a week, I was up six million and JB was gasping. It was hard to watch. I did something wild that maybe a trader wouldn't do today. A salesman was on the floor next to our desk. I liked him. Nice man, but not smart. A neat, well-groomed Englishman in his 40s. His name was Stanley Palmer. Stanley Palmer went nuts during the nuclear scare. At 11 a.m., he stood up on the trade floor and shouted, "THE NUKE RODS ARE EXPOSED!!!"

I heard desk juniors across the floor shouting the words to their desks. Titzy stood near me and shrieked, "THE NUKE RODS ARE EXPOSED!!!," hands around lips.

People raced back to their seats and yelled at their brokers and each other, creating a pandemonium. Stanley stood and said, "THE NUKE RODS ARE EXPOSED!!! Nuclear Rods Are Exposed!"

Like a clown, Titzy repeated it.

I told Titzy to stop talking.

Titzy shrugged and extended his hands wide like I was crazy.

"Titzy, what the fuck is a nuke rod?"

Titzy did the Italian hand gesture.

Stanley was still ranting when I returned.

What did I know about Stanley? I assumed he graduated from Oxford. What had he studied? Was it History? Was it Classics? Could it be PPE?

"No way, titzy. No way Stanley knows what a nuclear rod is."

Titzy didn't hear. He concentrated on his screens. JB screamed at his broker. He finally left his employment.

Pressing my Eurodollar broker button on the heavy brown phone. My palm covered my lips, and I sold tons of Eurodollar futures. My position changed. I now bet on rising rates, not calamity.

Avoid doing that. Don't change your mind on a whim. Avoid playing God—you're not invincible. But what will I say? I accomplished it at 24.

No nuclear plant exploded. Thank God.

Back up, I made five million more.

The finest trading is by smell. I smell idiocy.

Everyone was fucked afterward. Everyone stopped. I was heading the other way when JB stopped out at the worst possible time, at the peak of the pandemonium.

After everyone calmed down, I profited on all Eurodollars and predicted doom again. Despite not having a nuclear explosion in 2011, there would be one. I smelled it. In mid-April, I had nearly $11 million. Total desk height was less than ten. In red, JB was 1.7.

Being red isn't fun. Nobody likes it, but JB hated it.

A different generation JB. He was a good sportsman, talker, and charmer. He would have been a lawyer had he not quit Oxford. He wasn't a statistics or details person. Ground shifted under him.

Europe fell in 2011. Start with Greece. Spain, Italy, Portugal, Ireland followed. As predicted by the Prince, falling like dominoes. Nobody would lend or buy these governments' bonds. It helped me. Made lots of money.

National governments borrow from whom? It's mostly national banks. That's you, bank depositors. Banks lend deposits to governments.

That's fine—before 2011, economists regarded financing to governments "risk-free."

They erred.

Why are government loans risk-free? Governments can print money in an emergency, theoretically. If they fall into major difficulties and owe you a lot, they can print money to pay you.

Unfortunately, Italy cannot. Nor can Spain. Neither can Greece. Nor can Portugal. European governments lost the right to print money after the euro was created. These countries were always regarded as super-safe credits, so nobody worried. Until now.

When these countries went bankrupt in 2011, doubts were raised about whether their banks, which had lent to them and were owed significant amounts by their governments, were bankrupt too. Less than three years after Lehman. No one wants more bank failures. The ECB had to act.

Next, the ECB did something unusual. They gave all European banks unlimited 1% loans.

Central Banking rarely operates this way. Central banks prefer to get meticulous when setting interest rates. Banks' lending rates were usually strictly monitored. They would pump cheap money into the system to lower rates if they were too high. If rates were too low, they'd lend less or borrow back, raising the market rate. Thus, central banks controlled interest rates by influencing credit supply. Control quantity, control price. Similar to iPhones and Nikes.

Unlimited loans make it impossible to manage the amount. Without quantity management, you have no price control. To prevent banks failing, the ECB must have done it, but the markets went crazy.

A ridiculous ECB-commercial bank game. In its "auctions" for unlimited 1% loans, the ECB gave everyone exactly what they wanted, thus they weren't auctions. When it became apparent the Greek government was failing, banks flooded the auctions for loans. They borrowed so much that money flooded into the system, and European interest rates fell to zero, even less than zero on some days, a whole percentage point below the ECB's "official" interest rate of 1%, which served as the loan cost. Since interest rates had dropped to zero, few bought for ECB loans at the following auction. The market ran out of money, and rates rose above 2%. Each bank tried to calculate how much the others would borrow every week. If you knew everyone would borrow, you'd avoid it to get cheap money. You'd deposit as much cash as possible if other banks wouldn't borrow. Everyone tried to do what others didn't. The outcome was devastation.

Some weeks had numerous auctions. It was impossible to predict the daily interest rate. Sub-0% to 2% is possible. Days would swing wildly between those two extremes. Actually, I had no idea what was happening. That was fine because I had Titzy. Titzy pursued that crap everyday like a bloodhound.

JB lacked Titzy. JB was broke. JB was aging. Interest rates were never that high. In his time, the Central Bank established them monthly and left them alone. All our valuation and pricing algorithms were designed for that reality. JB couldn't adjust. My only responsibility was to price the front month—about 26–27 business days. It was only doable with Titzy manually updated daily. There was no other option. Twenty-three months awaited JB. About six hundred days. Out in his element.

He was battered daily. I knew his prices were wrong. HSBC trader Simon Chang, who had been promoted to euros, would ask me on the IB chat every day why I was showing inaccurate pricing.

"It's not me," I typed. It's JB."

"Why is JB showing the wrong prices? He will be steamed. Why not tell him!?

Good query. Why didn't I tell him?

***

Truthfully, I never thought of it. Why? Maybe that's my personality.

JB struggled. Struggling for air. Every day he lost money. Was killing it. Was creaming it. I made money on all of Titzy's prices, and my disaster position brought me cash every time I went on the floor. JB never turned to ask why.

In reality, he was rarely there.

Last few years were good to JB. They treated everyone at that desk well. Everyone made lots of money. So did I. JB had lived the dream too. Your share may have been done by him.

JB bought Thames-view luxury apartments. One secretary was pregnant by him. She was having his first child.

Often away from the desk. He had long broker lunches. He would return red-faced and spread himself on the markets like bugs on a windscreen. It hurt to watch.

I told Snoopy I was worried.

"Don't worry about JB," Snoopy smiled. "I know the wealthiest man." It goes, I suppose. So it goes.

***

JB was absent from the desk, so I covered. He spent more time away from the desk. Before the euro market went crazy, my short-dated euros book was the busiest on the desk by far. It was a constant, frantic rollercoaster, and I was doing more than half of JB's work. It was intense.

Well, what do you do? Can you do more? You labor. As Europe crashed, my PnL soared, and I spent 22 million in June. I was the floor's top trader by then. I was killing it in my big moment, and no Queensland drunkard would stop me.

I did my and JB's jobs. I started work early every day and made Titzy do the same. I jumped off my bike and onto the trade floor. I became the market leader by locking myself into screens, speaker boxes, headphones, beeps, and dings. I traded almost €500bn daily. I don't know how these things rank globally, but I'm probably one of the biggest traders. Traders had no choice in the wild market.

I forgot to change out of my bike clothing and eventually didn't care. Not even my work attire went to the office. I traded a gray hoodie, black fingerless gloves, and fading Onitsuka Tigers daily. I set up sound alerts on my computer to notify me of particular events. When my PnL reached another half-million bucks, my station went crazy and made "Ka-Ching" sounds. They would gain a lot. I would blast reggae music from my speakers on maximum volume on large win days, and

Titzy and I would put our feet up on the desks and drink two single espressos at a time while jamming out. Liquidator, Django Return, 54–46. I was the King of the Trading Floor and Titzy was my right-hand guy. Although Titzy wasn't making any money, he was pleased to go along for the ride as a youngster. What, he was a kid? I'm younger than Titzy. Each of us was 24. I dreamed about markets every night at home.

***

Have you ever been called arrogant?

JB had returned from the bathroom. After using the restroom, JB always ramped.

I was tired of JB's crap. Man never comes, sets inaccurate rates, and loses money daily. After giving his meager earnings to brokers, he calls me arrogant.

I ignored him. I focused on my mouse while his gaze burned into my left cheek. Respectfully, I removed my Bluetooth headset's left earpiece.

"No. Never. Nobody ever."

"Well. That's surprising. Don't you think that's arrogant?

I pulled a blue ballpoint pen from my drawer and tapped it on the plasticky desk. I considered splitting it but decided against it. I set it down and faced JB.

"JB, when will you get out of the red?"

Less than a foot separated our faces. When his nose's shattered blood vessels spread across his face like an illness, I remembered how much the man had helped me and felt horrible for saying what I did. But my face didn't reveal it.

"Don't worry. It's happened before and will again. I know my stuff."

"The trade, then? Come on JB. Trade what?

JB examined my eyes and I examined his. Now our faces were almost touching, and I could hear his slow, measured breathing. The pure blueness of an old man's eyes that had seen the world for years caught my attention. The silence was long. I wasn't sure if he was reading or thinking. Not sure if I was reading him.

"Stocks."

"Stocks?"

"Stocks," JB said insistently.

Stocks are traded?

"Stocks. These are too high."

"Stocks are too high?"

Look at them! They're too damn high! They've barely fallen and the economy will tank! They must descend."

I looked away from JB and tapped the pen twenty times on the empty desk.

"JB, you don't understand? That doesn't work. Stocks never fall. Stocks always rise. When the economy is healthy, stocks rise, and when it's bad, they create more money, raising them. Same with fucking houses. Everything rises. Asset holders always win. Rich people always win. Only the rich win. Buy fucking stocks, mate. Going to the moon. You'll be great, mate. Do not worry."

I bought four single espressos.

***

Gotta be honest. When JB was off the desk, I quoted his prices and mine without as much effort. His rates were in his book and PnL. Pricing was in my book and mine. I prioritized. Sorry, I did.

JB knew. Blowup was inevitable.

Remember that market makers take the spread. Say the real price is 71. I quote 70–72, you purchase at 72, I find a seller at 71, and we're done. You bought what you wanted, I profited. Everyone's glad.

Unfortunately, there is no true price. It's constantly shifting. What if it moves without your notice?

Say it's 74 now. Some stuff happened when I was pissed. Due to his hectic schedule, Morley hasn't changed the price on his screen yet. You phone me for a price. The screen shows 70–72. I say 70–72. I want to buy at 71 and you lift me at 72.

The price from Morley is 73–75.5.

Fuck.

I can't go without losing 3.5.

Tell Morley I'll pay 73.

Too late. Someone else bids 74."

"Fuck it, still have the 75.5 offer? I'll pay 75."

Two minutes silent.

Sorry mate, 75.5 is gone. Best I have is 77."

See, market-making is hard. You must carefully consider when you pisses.

***

Off-desk JB. He was drinking beer, sake, raw seafood, and who knows what else.

I was busy when someone called about JB pricing. What was I doing? No idea. Maybe I was choosing dinner that night. I was practicing duck à l'orange.

Quickly set your cookbook on the table and open your price screen. Ask a broker, "Where are three months?"

"34–37."

34–37, that sounds right, tell the salesman.

"34–37."

"37 mine, 2 yards."

As the salesman hangs up, the speakerbox crackles with radio distortion.

2 yards. That's a lot. We should probably start with some. Switch to the broker.

"Marco. Are you still there after three months?

Still there. 34–37."

"Mine. One yard."

Crackle. Two and a half minutes silence. You see price adjustments on your computer screen. 35–38. 36–39. Fucking Marco, no 37 offer. Absolute nonsense.

"Marco, where's my fucking three months?"

"Mate I regret it's gone; my best is 39."

"Fuck! Why did you tell me you had 37 then?"

"Mate I was fucking let down."

Forget him—he never had it. I knew immediately it was gone.

I updated JB PnL. He lost 100K. Just recently, he had reached profitability. That would almost put him in the red again. I lean on Titzy.

"Titzy!"

"Hmph!?"

Titzy ate lasagna from a cardboard box with a plastic fork.

"Titzy, I got hit by JB in three months and it's gone. He lost 100. What shall we do?

"Fuck, he just broke zero. Might you cover it?

"If we cover it now, he'll lose $200 and be in the red. You think? You should text him."

I wrote JB a text.

"You were hit in three months. It dropped 100K."

I refreshed his PnL before texting. It dropped 200. Instead of "It's down 100K," I wrote "It's not looking good."

The text was sent.

***

When JB returned to the desk at 4 p.m., the deal was down 400K. JB looked thrilled and like he would fall over. It was obvious he hadn't read the text. Right, Titzy was looking at me. I turned up two of my shirt's three buttons. As did Titzy. My PC was silenced. Inappropriate time for ka-ching.

"How's the world looking, fuckers?"

JB sat down. His PnL was updated. I tried not to look at him, but I saw his face bleed. His reflex was to press Marco's button.

Marco, where's three months?

Crackle. Pause. "41–44."

"What the hell is this?"

I overlooked JB and focused on his speakerbox. The Marco light was off. He was speaking to me.

It's three months, mate. In three months, you were hit. As stated in the text, I informed you. Is the text not visible?

I had him. He missed the text. It was clear he hadn't seen the text. We both knew he should.

JB stood slowly and reached for his pocket. He brandished his phone like a rifle. Word-by-word, he read the text.

In three months, you got hit. It doesn't look good."

JB placed his phone down and stood, so I did too. We squared when he faced me. JB shoved the final three words in my face.

Looks bad. Not…looking…good."

I thought about that.

"Well... Is it not true?

JB pursed his lips and nodded hastily.

You'll do what?

He said what was evident. Over 24 million dollars. That transaction hurt JB. I'm sure JB would have accepted the exchange.

My first meeting with JB came to mind. How he welcomed me. He was the first trader on the desk to talk to me and gave me my first book. He consoled me after I lost $8 million. I recalled his words— "tough times don't last, tough people do." Looking into his crimson face, I imagined four magnificent flats facing Big Ben.

I bit hard on my cheek with my tongue deep in.

"Tough times pass JB. People are tough."

***

JB exploded. He threw his hefty brown phone into his displays at full speed. The phone hit his central screen directly in the middle, buckled and broke, and bounced harmlessly onto his desk. Nothing broke. Screens have changed, I suppose. I remember thinking the whole movement, which was quick, decisive, and athletic, produced too little sound.

JB seemed as unhappy as I was. He slammed the phone into his desk at least seven or eight times, each time with an Australian "fuck."

The noise output was significantly better.

During a brief quiet, everyone gazed at JB and JB looked ahead. He kept the phone in his right hand. His left hand groped for his speakerbox and his right held the phone to his ear again, almost reflexively.

"Robbie, where's three months?"

He hit another broker's button.

Robin, where are three months?

A short pause, then a FUCK and BANG as the phone hit the desk hard. It was satisfying.

"Timmie Where's three months? FUCK!

"Millzy, where's three months? FUCK!" Bang!

He walked down the broker lines one by one. It was beautiful and musical.

"JB WHAT'S UP?"

Chuck put his hands around his lips and was crying out to JB naturally, as if the ruckus were external. JB was too busy to respond.

"GARY, WHAT'S UP?"

The question was difficult to answer. My thoughts raced over various answers. I chose "I THINK JB'S PHONE IS BROKEN."

I believed it to be factual.

Chuck nodded with understanding, as if JB's reaction was the only reasonable response to being a trader with a malfunctioning phone, and got up. He gently strolled by JB and me to a tiny supply cupboard at the other end of the desk. He struggled to the bottom draw and produced a massive, heavy brown handphone with a long, twisted cord.

I'll never comprehend Chuck's next move. Instead of passing the phone to JB, he exclaimed, "HERE YOU GO JB."

Throwing the phone in the air.

I thought it moved slowly. A high, arcing toss hit the trading floor's high ceiling. It peaked to my right above Titzy's head. Titzy starred. I dodged and retreated as it fell above me.

No need—Chuck never missed. The phone fell precisely on JB's bald head.

I waited. Everyone waited. Suddenly, the trade floor was quiet. I feared JB would kill Chuck.

But he didn't. He paused. He was inactive. Stopped pressing buttons. His phone bashing stopped. He softly reclined in his chair and looked to think profoundly. It was always an option to flick up a switch to one of his brokers instead of using the buttons, which allowed him to connect without his broken phone.

"Where's three months?"

"41–44."

Can you get me two yards at 44?

A pause, then "Yes, do you want it?"

"My 2 yards. 44."

JB then did nothing. He sat and breathed deeply for five minutes. He touched the top of his head with his right hand and then glanced at his fingers for blood. He got up and headed home.

I thought beating somebody on the head wouldn't make them smart. I thought only cartoons did that. Maybe you can.

Chuck's third-last act.

***

Harry fretted at home. Not going out. All I did was cook and make money.

Harry heard my name around the market. My fame was growing. Harry didn't understand why I didn't enjoy it. Actually, neither could I. He would invite my friends around to drink and try to get me to go clubbing. He surprised me with a party and an expensive Cargo VIP table on my birthday. I pretended to use the restroom, then escaped and rode the bus home.

Harry kept talking to me, and I could tell he meant well. Finally, I said we could go to one party. The Matchstick Factory where we lived was hosting a summer event. Some girl was smiling at me at the gym down there, so I assumed she'd go. I wanted to demonstrate to the kid I was still capable.

She was with her friend when we went. I offered a one-liter Bacardi and asked if they wanted to drink. Apparently they did. I'm no charmer, but I can drop a move.

The four of us went to a bar late, past my bedtime. Since my eyelids were drooping and Harry liked her, I decided to let it go. We took a night bus home after I asked her flatmate, a friend, to go to

McDonald's. After sitting on the bus, I fell asleep and woke up to her stroking my hair.

***

It was summer when Snoopy married. Bill was the only one invited to the wedding.

Chuck asked, "How's married life treating ya!?" while I was in the corner attempting to convince Snoopy that economic recovery wouldn't happen.

He had to twist and arch his neck since Chuck was behind Snoopy, who was sitting.

"Ermmm… Chuck, it's okay. It's okay... So good!"

What do you mean it's good? Give details!"

"I don't know Chuck, what should I say? Very good! She cooks dinner for me after a long day at work. Very nice!"

That upset Chuck.

"What does she cook for you?"

"What does she cook for me? She cooks something new daily!"

"Well… She cooked you what last night?

Snoop contemplated.

"Last night, she baked pasta."

Chuck wrinkled his forehead and face. He rubbed his head and looked away.

"Pasta?," he exclaimed. Again, "Pasta!?"

He leaned down on the desk to look at Snoopy and questioned, "Pasta…with curry?!?" with childlike sincerity.

Snoopy and I chuckled about that for a while, taking a break from the desk.

Chuck's second-last act.

***

Something about her. I consider her a wizard."

Harry drunkenly described her like way. I took the bus home with the party girl. Wizard was her nickname afterward.

Wizard had long, straight, blond hair, enormous green eyes, and white complexion. She was pale blue by moonlight.

81

I described my job.

"It doesn't sound like you like it much," she told me.

'What do you mean I dislike it? Of course I enjoy it!"

"If you don't like it, quit. I'd do that."

"Look, I'm not looking for anything serious," I said. I doubt I'll last. I have to go somewhere, but I don't know where. I recommend finding someone else."

***

Chuck called us into a room. Since I was no longer the desk junior, I could enter the room. Titzy was on the desk.

Sunlight filled the room. Chuck always got the greatest accommodations. Chuck was at the head of a long table with the window behind him. Standing next to JB. Bill and Snoopy sat opposite us. Other dealers were scattered.

Chuck reported getting lost on the way home two weeks prior. Chuck stated he had been lost before. But it was the first time his wife knew, and she hospitalized him. Chuck had a tennis-ball-sized brain tumor.

"I've got to take some time off work."

JB pressed his elbow into my upper arm and I could feel his warmth through my sleeve as Billy stared at me.

"But it's fine. Doctors say they can remove it. So I shouldn't be away from the desk for long."

With that, my eyes returned to Chuck's dark shadow beside the window, his thick spectacles, his broad smile, and his father-like hairstyle. Chuck never did that again. Never saw Chuck again.

2

FROG Sat Me Down in Room.

Slug says, "You can't have the sabbatical."

Don't reply. Just nod.

"He said the last sabbatical recipient never returned. He doesn't want that for you."

Nod again.

Another possibility exists. Caleb returns. He will lead STIRT Tokyo. He wants you over there."

One more nod.

"What do you think?"

Sigh deeply. Stop and think.

I don't think it's a good idea, Frog. Fucked. I'm done."

Time for the Frog to sigh. He cracked his knuckles while pretending to think for himself and looking down. Later he looked at me with a frown wider than his hideous face.

Gary, you don't get it. Get going."

OK.

No issue.

So it goes.

***

My dad and I went to a posh Japanese restaurant in the City to announce my move to Japan.

They dressed for church and shuffled ceaselessly in the stool-like high chairs.

Will you be safe outside?

My mother.

Yes, I will. I'm always fine."

I assumed they didn't know how to handle chopsticks because they couldn't destarch continuously.

"It's okay," I informed them, "you can eat sushi with your hands."

I took one and ate it to prove it was allowed. But my dad was doing something strange with the soy sauce bottle, so he missed it.

I requested two forks from the waitress. Nothing seemed to help.

***

Two weeks before leaving, I planned to tell the Wizard we should break up.

When I spoke about it, we were in bed and it was deep blue.

"Hey… You know I'm heading to Japan?

Yes, I know you're going."

I sat above her bed. The room was filled with blue with all the drapes open. I saw her words in the air and tried to catch them. I remembered something I was meant to say or do, but I couldn't remember what, so she filled the vacuum.

"Don't you know I'm going too? You know I'll visit Japan?

I heard a voice from another room, waking me up. I looked down and thought, "You know I don't deserve you." You should find someone else."

However, I stated, "I think I need…you to come."

It wasn't my plan, so I don't know why I said that. I probably said that because it was true.

***

My last day on the Citibank London trading floor was late September 2012. Bag up. Pat some backs. JB exclaimed, "Gary Stevenson is leaving the building!" as I left the desk.

I left the room knowing they were shouting and clapping. I could hear and see them down every aisle and both sides in my peripheral vision. Pink, blue, white, and white shirts.

I left without looking back.

PART FOUR
THERMOSTAT

1

Tokyo is great for depression. Especially fall.

The banks gather at a region of the city called "Marunouchi," which means "inside the circle," because it was once part of the Emperor's palace's outer moat, but I don't know where it is anymore. I never found it.

High buildings in Marunouchi were forbidden for a long time because they could overlook the palace and be used to shoot the Emperor with a crossbow. But in the 1980s, the land value rose so high that exceptions were created, and by the time I arrived, the whole region was fifty floors high. Yes, tradition and the Emperor matter, but so does money.

Walking west from the Citi office building, the dark gray and metal Shin-Marubiru, I could enter the palace's Outer Garden, "Koukyogaien." This garden is an immense, immaculately maintained area divided into three sections by two busy roads and planted with a million individual but identical trees spaced seven or eight meters apart.

Each tree is little, around a man's height, and complex, like nothing I've seen in England. When I initially entered the garden, I thought these were bonsai trees, but I subsequently realized that bonsai is a Japanese artform of tiny-tree cultivation, not a tree. So I guess they're another type of Japanese tree.

An historic stone bridge bridges the inner moat and leads to the inner part of the Imperial Palace complex after 10 minutes of walking through the gardens past the million distinct, identical trees. The gate is always closed, so you can't enter.

I regularly went there, sat on a dirt step, and watched Marunouchi. You gain perspective there. Tokyo's skyscrapers rise into the azure sky, and the Koukyogaien's green field and trees are in the foreground. Canary Wharf is not Marunouchi. I watched Canary Wharf's few towers rise one by one. I see them as persons, notably the Citibank Tower, HSBC Tower, and pyramid one, which I watched rise as a child. Marunouchi has more skyscrapers than not. At least thirty, forty, or fifty forty-story buildings must have stood together as a block. The sky in my memory is always warm and blue, even though Tokyo's weather changes greatly from summer to winter. That may be because that's how it was when I arrived in late September 2012.

I always thought the same thing as I observed Marunouchi on the short step outside the Emperor's Palace.

"My God," I thought, "there are so many windows."

Skyscrapers with several stories and windows. Behind each window are rows and rows of men and women working on computers from morning to night.

How have they not solved the world's problems?

I would stand up, dust the white gravel filth from my trousers, and stroll back to my office, where I would wager on the end of the world.

2

When I moved to Tokyo, I shouldn't have. After months of losing weight, I was under 60 kilograms, or nine and a half stone. Even for me, that's little.

I doubt I realized I had an issue. I once thought it was odd to be pathologically unable to buy sofas or other furnishings. I let it pass, as I did with many uncertain moments. If I hadn't done it, things might not have become so bad so fast. There were other serious matters, like interest rates.

PPIs, which prevent stomach acid from being acidic, were treating my heart pain. The first time I took them a year ago, they relieved the pain.

After three courses, they weren't working as well when I moved to Japan. I questioned the doctor, "Is that it?" Just take these medications forever?

He grinned and added, "Probably." as he handed me the prescription.

I traded through it all. Trading, trading, trading. My only true friend remained. Unaffected, safe.

Trading is always present. The markets keep going.

They cease on weekends, but the economy still exists.

The economy became my preoccupation, spreading like oil into my heart's acid.

It was true that I no longer cared about work. But the economy? That love endured.

I didn't think much about it when I realized the economy was broken and would become worse every year. I considered it, of course. I never pondered its meaning.

My work, you know? You look at the economy and wonder what it will be this year. The economy: strong or weak? What about next year? That simplifies it, but interest rates trading is just that. That was my job.

Say you measured pool depths. You would not measure pools and ask, "What does this mean?," would you? Imagine fixing sofas was your job. Never ask friends, "What does this sofa mean?"

When I knew the economy would always worsen, I was confident. I was confident enough to bet big. I understood how it would happen and why most economists would miss it. I saw it clearly. I still see it. Never questioned myself, "What does it mean?"

Just traded. Just performed my job.

As that move made me Citi Global Foreign Exchange's most lucrative trader, I realized this was more than a hypothesis. This was real.

I got paid a lot for that and invested it. When investing, I wondered, "What am I investing this money for?" Will I ever spend it? Likely not."

I thought, "Well, in that case, I'm investing it for my kids."

Suddenly, "But what if I'm right?" In what universe will my kids live?

I rejected the thinking and quickly returned to investing because I loved numbers. I feel safe with numbers.

Moments existed, nevertheless. Short moments. I glimpsed a dark, starry sky through the heavy canopy of trees above me. In those instances, I considered resigning. That probably happened in the workplace with the Frog that day. In one scorching moment of awareness, I glimpsed the sky and recognized that a billionaire twenty-five-year-old shouldn't work with holes in his shoes or live in a house without floors. Sleeping on a broken crimson sofa in the evenings and waking up cold, dreaming numbers. He had shooting heart pains and sometimes couldn't eat. That's probably why I indicated I wanted to resign then.

Inability to quit was the issue. I was handcuffed in. Citibank did everything they could to keep me glued to my screens when they gave me that hefty bonus at the start of 2012. My investment money was part of the bonus received upfront. The rest would be paid far behind. Quarters in 2013, 2014, 2015, and 2016. At that point, I couldn't leave. My bank owes me almost £1 million. If I resigned, I'd lose everything. I probably answered yes when the Frog informed me I had to move to Tokyo since I was there in that office with my broken shoes, stomach, and heart, feeling low and like a rat. Despite knowing I lacked the energy. I had nothing. No refusal power. I was chained.

We both have teeth, rats and me. I researched in my own time.

How did Caleb depart in 2009 if merchants are shackled? How had Caleb built it? His beautiful mansion in the trees?

Explored and asked individuals. I just asked Bill.

Bill told me the contract had a clause to leave and keep your money. You had to leave for charitable work. Although few knew about it, Caleb did and activated that provision. Everyone knew he'd never worked for charity, but the Slug let him go. The reason was unknown. There was uncertainty. Maybe Caleb shit on the Slug.

I carried this thin escape rope on that lengthy journey alone to Tokyo. If Caleb went with his money, I could too. Also, I would work for

Caleb. If everything went wrong, I'd wait until the next bonus and go to work for charity. Caleb must realize that, right?

He would, obviously. This Caleb would grasp.

***

I was alone on that Tokyo aircraft. The Wizard was absent. The Wizard promised to move to Japan, but she didn't when I did. She booked a flight and a job outside Tokyo, which didn't start until January 2013.

I brought almost nothing. I got eight cubic meters of air freight from the bank to transport my favorite furniture? I asked them to deliver my bike because I scarcely had anything bigger than a backpack. However, my bike took two weeks to arrive, leaving me, my luggage, and the marketplaces.

I no longer saw numbers in markets then or now. I saw world projections, like a weather forecast. Interest rate estimates showed when and how fast each economy would recover, and they changed daily. If rates fall, economic prospects may have diminished or the central bank may have announced they won't raise rates. Which is it? The stock market shows that the first reason will likely lower equities and the second, raise them.

Real traders follow markets, not news. Fuck The Economist, Financial Times, and Wall Street Journal. You merely need marketplaces. Real information will be given.

But it's wrong. It exists. It's wrong. I was figuring out why. My economic predictions have only been correct a year and a half. I needed to see more to test my theories. I wanted confirmation. I needed to see the economy crash.

So that was my plan. Even with a half-empty rucksack, I knew I could always trade and make money. I wanted another year of accurate predictions. I sought God's truth.

I wanted nothing else. Nothing except marketplaces.

3

Pink shirts weren't popular in Tokyo when I went. No blue shirts. White-shirt culture prevails. At 8 and 9 a.m., white shirts, neatly bordered by black trousers and slim black suit jackets, cascade out of underground station exits like waterfalls into the real world, and the men and women inside are carp fighting upstream, opening umbrellas, checking their phones, carrying neat, prim, rectangular suitcases, and mopping their brows with small white handkerchiefs.

I was there.

Citibank handled everything. I received a crisp, cream, and white apartment on the thirtieth story of the Prudential Building, a tower where insurance should be sold but where the top corner has been designated for human habitation. In the top corner, courageous adventurers like myself sleep and wake up every night high in the sky, seeing Mount Fuji every morning, but the windows are supposed to stay closed, so we don't breathe Tokyo's high air.

The Prudential Building connects to the vast, sprawling, and efficient Tokyo subway system at Akasaka Mitsuke station, in the heart of Akasaka, an upmarket commercial district in central Tokyo with old-fashioned sushi shops, narrow paved alleys, and high rents.

I could take an elevator from the hallway outside my bedroom all the way down to the station, where I could take the Marunouchi line in eight minutes to Tokyo Station and then another elevator directly into my office. I never saw the sky from my bed to the trading floor. You believe it's convenient? As the Japanese say, "便利ですね?"

***

The Tokyo trading floor on the twenty-fourth story of the Shin-Maru-Biru (New Marunouchi Building) was large. I thought it was small. To see the back of the room and its right and left sides at once, stand with

90

your back straight and against the entrance door and your head touching it. That meant it was small to me.

Its low ceilings and silence likely made it feel small. The room's altitude generated a vastness through the windows on the two sides that did not face the Marunouchi buildings. For some reason, Tokyo's sky seemed abnormally high from my first day in the office.

Unusually high and quiet. Those impressions stunned me. The floor was expensively carpeted, so you couldn't hear a pin drop. But I always thought you could.

The trade floor included a few pink shirts, which gave comfort and familiarity. Not because Japanese traders were fashionably adventurous, but because the trading floor featured a lot of gaijin. Gaijin—foreigner. Kind of signifies white and American. Not usually derogatory. It happens sometimes.

About a third of the trading floor was gaijin, and two thirds were Americans. The remainder were lost Europeans. People like me. Only Caleb and two Japanese traders, Hisa Watanabe and Joey Kanazawa, whom I had met on my globe trip nearly two years before, were familiar to me on the trading floor.

The STIRT desk was at the back of the trading floor beside the far window, so I could look out at the palace if I chose. I don't have a crossbow, so no biggie. There were only three traders, including me, and only one ever traded, so calling it a desk was misleading.

In Asia, Citi STIRT was split between Tokyo and Sydney. Sydney exchanged all currencies except the Japanese yen, which was traded in Japan. This meant Tokyo needed only one trader, a Japanese currency dealer. But there we were, three of us, in a small line: Hisa Watanabe, Arthur Kapowski, and me, packed between them.

As long as anyone could remember, Hisa Watanabe traded yen. He was a terrible trader and strangely spoke English with a 1920s New York gangster accent. He was little and mousy. Not fair. He didn't trade. He was a shopkeeper, accountant, and paper-pusher.

Hisa should have been dismissed when I got his position. He wasn't. I got his chair and he moved right and became "my manager." I'm my own manager. Hisa, his wife, and crying infant met me at the Tokyo airport when I arrived. I didn't understand what that meant when it happened. He would backseat drive my trading unerringly and relentlessly, sticking up my arsehole like a hemorrhoid for six months. On my left was Arthur Kapowski. Arthur was Australian and his father was a mining mogul, star plastic surgeon, or newspaper tycoon. Perhaps someone anonymously affluent and prominent, and it appeared that he had raised his son to be the next clear leader of the Australian Republican Party. He looked like the world's tallest and most prestigious fifteen-year-old, but he was probably twenty-five. Imagine Jared Kushner with a better trainer. I never met a more right-wing individual than Arthur. Arthur excelled. He was hilarious.

Arthur was only in Tokyo because Rupert Hobhouse, Clapham's wolfman, was still head of STIRT in Asia and loved to move people around like chess pieces. Arthur may have been put there to assist me settle in or so Rupert could brag to Caleb that he had employed a future global leader as his junior trader on STIRT. Arthur appeared happy to be there. It was closer to his lover. The girlfriend lives in NYC.

We were the three STIRT "traders"—the trader, his boss, and his subordinate. Three fucking cooks and little broth.

As if three men for one task weren't enough, Rupert, "my boss" from 5,000 miles away, demanded a live video screen between his and my workstation. This meant that one of my precious screens was now permanently dedicated to a rolling livestream of "Rupert's daily moments," including "Rupert eats noodles too quickly," "Rupert perfects the art of the full windsor necktie," and "Rupert suddenly unmutes his screen to shout at you 'What's Eurozone CPI?' like some fucking horrible recurring dream from childhood which has inexplicably come back to haunt you as an adult."

The Foreign Exchange section was left of us. The Tokyo FX team was too small to split into separate desks, so we shared our desk with a pair of thoroughly unobjectionable middle-aged Japanese salesmen who, as my Japanese improved, spent their entire day discussing what they would eat for lunch and then a thorough assessment of it. The semi-legendary and violently irrepressible Joey Kanazawa was one of two Japanese currency traders past them, and to their left, on the end of the desk, was the broad and robust Caleb Zucman, who had been made head of the foreign-exchange-and-interest-rates department and propped up the desk like the world's largest bookend, bringing the number of bosses in my immediate vicinity to three. Sure, I'd be taken care of.

4

Japanese have a concept called O-mo-te-na-shi. Some Japanese repeat it one syllable at a time and perform this crazy thing with their hands. Apparently, it implies "the spirit of Japanese hospitality." I think green tea is involved.

It may not have been O-mo-te-na-shi, but Joey Kanazawa showed me Japanese hospitality. I suppose it was different.

Joey Kanazawa was petite, had keen eyes, and moved efficiently. A "spot trader," he traded currencies exclusively. The easiest trader, they are known for being dumb and impolite. All traders call FX traders monkeys, and FX traders call spot traders monkeys. Thus, they are monkeys of monkeys. Joey Kanazawa was different. He was cool, stylish, and quiet.

My first day on the trading floor, Joey spoke little to me or anyone else. At 6:30 p.m., he stood up, moved his chair in, took three steps to his right, and shouted something in Japanese.

The three Japanese guys around me—Hisa Watanabe and the two lunch connoisseurs—responded with a violent grunt and protracted hiss. They got up and sat individually.

The four men moved balletically together. I stared at Joey, shocked and pleased.

Joey put his right arm straight towards me. With his palm up and thumb, index, and middle fingers extended, he pointed a rifle. He kept my state briefly with seething eyes. Rip the rifle into the air.

The gesture was decisive and broke our separate language. I searched beneath my desk for my string backpack and followed him into the night.

***

Late September in Tokyo was dark, and the final blue was fading from the air.

The sky turns black and streets glow. The stars fell.

I now realize we must have been going through Ginza, one of Tokyo's and the world's most prestigious retail avenues, east of Marunouchi.

Before I knew what I know now, I saw only a great, broad street with gorgeous trees and tall buildings. Numerous unreadable neon signs cascading from building sides. with two pairs, four Japanese men with white shirts and black coats walk. Broken white trainers, thin black Topman peacoat—me—behind them, looking around, upward.

***

That first sweltering Tokyo evening, following those four white-shirted men into the darkness, what was I looking for? Maybe I wanted omotenashi. The Japanese hospitality spirit. Every silly little white lad who packs it all in and moves to Japan wants that, right? Being held by a fresh, distinct area and embraced by its warm air.

A abrupt right into an unsuitable alley barely large enough for two people. Four males at a hot red counter slurping noodles together, one boy dropping his. I asked Hisa how to say "black pepper" in Japanese. He called it "burakku peppaa." A little walk, another tiny alley. Five men in a lift. No one told me where we were headed. After that, it went downhill.

Hostess bars, soaplands, and karaoke—what can I say? Very likely more than any of us wants to know. Just women. So many women. Did I state I wasn't warned?

There were older and younger women. Really girls. There were Wizard-aged women. Huge, decorated rooms and smaller, private rooms were available. Allocation. Lot of allotment. I always get one.

Smoked cigarettes, drank mixed beverages, and chuckled at jokes behind hands. Unfortunately, I cannot speak Japanese. Laughter, thigh touch.

That situation—what do you do? Maybe I should have gone home. But I didn't. Why not?

I waited and drank slowly, but the cups were always full, making it hard to measure. Connoisseurs now wore ties. My furendo. She izu. Staa Adaruto.

We're tumbling into taxis and heading to the next spot as it blurs. Joey Kanazawa leaps from his seat like a savage and rips the man's shirt from his chest while Hisa sings "Wonderwall." Nearby girl is pulling on my shoulder. She looks 20. She looks lovely. Unfortunately, I cannot speak Japanese.

I try to leave her, and she looks uncomfortably at the door's small porthole, so I look too. A man is watching us, and within minutes, the door opens, my girl goes, and another is sent in for me.

I apologize for my lack of Japanese, but I am fine and do not require anyone. I don't know how this works, but you can do what you want or go home."

She can't hear because the music is too loud and the connoisseurs are screaming a traditional Japanese ballad into the microphone, so I lean in and say the same thing into her ear. She smiles, puts her hand on my shoulder, and tilts her head to the side. She was replaced four more times.

If anything remained, my spirit died a little on that carousel. Eventually, an English-speaking female found me. She should have been listed higher.

"Please don't let them replace you."

Pureezu, pureezu. Be…More…Happy."

It occurred to me that I had never tried that. Maybe it was too late.

5

"SO. You made so much money—how?

Arthur was different from other traders I'd worked with, as shown by his query. I had been one of Citi's top traders for nearly two years, yet no one had asked me that.

"Easy. I bet interest rates will always be zero."

"HA!"

Arthur laughed raucously. One snide Australian privileged school laugh.

"Interest rates can't stay zero forever."

Arthur asked many stupid questions and made big assertions. I enjoyed it. He did this because he never studied economics. He studied music. He was a concert pianist or something. The finest profession for a concert pianist nowadays is Citibank trader. It pays well.

Students today never truly understand economics because their teachers, who were once economics students, never did either. In a rare moment of clarity, a student will be smart enough to realize their lack of comprehension and daring enough to question a lecturer. The professor, who has spent years trying to hide his lack of understanding of his subject, will feel a fleeting twinge of psychological pain and remember that his father has never been proud of him. As intellectually insecure people do when questioned, the professor would shame or bore his interlocutor into submission to repress these escaping feelings. This technique teaches economists to avoid asking dumb questions, which are usually the most essential.

Arthur was good at piano and didn't have that. How lucky. Lucky boy. Yes, interest rates can stay zero forever. Why heck can't they?

"Well…" Arthur contemplated this. Nice boy, you could tell he thought.

Because it's temporary. The sovereign debt problem. The economy will revive. Interest rates will return. Where did you read that? The economy is tanking."

"HA!"

This boy laughed loudly and enjoyed it. Everything he did was loud. When Arthur talked, everyone could hear him on the Tokyo trade floor, the quietest I've ever been on by a million miles. Arthur didn't care. Should he care? He'll lead the free globe.

"The economy's going to hell?"

"You think I mean what? It never improves. Terminal, not interim. Downhill from here. Year after year."

"What falls? Interest rates? The stock market?"

Fucking stock market, Arthur, you're wiser than that. Have you been sleeping for five years? Shit economy helps stocks. Stock market goes to moon."

I made a good point. It was getting clearer. Arthur nibbled.

"But why is the economy fucked? Nobody claims that. Why fucked?"

"Fucking hell Arthur. Believe what everyone else believes and you'll never make a pound. You can't beat the market by being it. When they are wrong, you profit."

Arthur seemed confused, and I wondered if he should be in a symphony hall instead of here with me.

"OK, continue. Fucking tell you. That's inequity. That's all that matters. Trade that and become a millionaire."

Arthur laughed one last time before understanding I was serious.

"Inequality!?"

Yes, Arthur, inequity. Poor people pay their entire wage to the rich every year to live in a house since the rich get the assets and the poor get the debt. The rich buy the remainder of the middle class's assets with that money, making the problem worse every year. The middle class goes, spending power evaporates forever, the affluent get richer, and the poor die.

I saw his brain cogs move while that lingered in the air.

"So… How about interest rates?

"Interest rates remain zero."

"Hmm… Should we buy green Eurodollars?

Fucking Arthur. Smarter than he seemed.

Rupert, as usual, was able to watch us on his video screen during the talk. He was unfortunately fond of unmuting the television and shouting my name.

"Gary! Glad you're doing well with Arthur! You talking about what? I was finding it harder to hide my disgust for Rupert at that point. Rupert probably didn't notice. Probably assumed all faces looked like that. I failed to respond due to a twitch in my eye and mouth, so Arthur exclaimed, "Economics!"

"Ahh…economics! I adore economics! I knew Gary would be a terrific economist. So I recruited him to the bank! Tell me, Gary... Who is Citibank's top economist?

Although Rupert was one of seven people claiming to have hired me at the bank, I thought his claim was stronger. Eventually, he took me to Vegas. After calming my eyes, I spat "Bill."

Shocked, Rupert.

"Bill is no economist!" He assumed I was joking.

"OK. If not Bill, me."

With joy, Rupert and Arthur chuckled at that. I could see Arthur's dazzling smile through our camera inlay in the corner of the screen showing Rupert. Rupert had his teeth done since arriving in Australia. Perfect like piano keys.

Caleb's face loomed behind me in the television frame and his hefty hand touched my shoulder.

"Rupert! How're things? Why are you folks so happy?

"Caleb! How're you? Just conversing with Gary. He claims to be the bank's best economist!"

Everyone laughed with their teeth and cheeks, including Caleb.

However, he is a competent economist. Since the Trading Game, I knew he would be. So I hired him for the bank." Caleb paused to rebalance and proceed with additional gravity.

"I'll never forget giving Gary his first bonus. Whatever I offered him would be a lot of money, but I wanted him to feel appreciated. I'll never forget his face when we presented him with £50,000."

The three men smiled warmly and glanced at me while I stared at the screens. It was £13,000, not £50,000, and I pondered why Caleb would lie so boldly to a man who knew it was a falsehood. Three massive, beautiful smiles. Not smiling, I looked like a rodent.

***

I made a lot of money and won Arthur's devotion when global interest rates collapsed one last time. I probably suffered the worst.

When interest rate estimates drop to zero, everyone's right. Each person is right. For the first time in nearly two years since taking the job, everyone agreed with me. Economy sucked forever. Nobody would recover. Being right and everyone agreeing is the worst. No money may be made.

I was a global trading powerhouse just months prior. I traded hundreds of billions daily in a volatile market. That ended. I traded yen. For an American bank. Not a Japanese bank. Japanese interest rates never moved, and the market was lifeless. Even with pricing, Hisa overruled them and I couldn't fight back.

All done. No trading game customers. No economy to bet on dying. Just me, Arthur, Hisa Watanabe, and two men discussing lunch.

No trades. First time in a while, no trades. While using the mouse and keyboard, I noticed how empty my hands were.

Turning right, I looked. There was Hisa Watanabe. He slurped noodles from a cardboard bowl with chopsticks, sounding horrible. I shouldn't detest Hisa Watanabe too much. I know why he did it. Backseat driving and overriding my trades. It wasn't good for him that I was there, doing his job, and making more money than ever without working. Man's wife married him for his merchant salary, and he needed to keep it. He wasn't the first trader in that situation. Fuck him, but good luck.

I looked left. Arthur Kapowski. Kid loved all our money from betting on the end of the world. I wondered whether it had ever made me happy like it did him. God knows those suffering looked like my parents, not his.

I checked my top-left screen. Rupert Hobhouse. By chance, the guy was likewise eating noodles from a cardboard bowl. I was grateful his television was on mute. My first realization was that I despised him. Did I loathe or despise him? No idea, what's the difference? I pondered why and whether he knew I disliked him. God knows he helped me

99

professionally. He made me loathe him more as he helped me. It goes, I suppose.

Left again, past Arthur, to connoisseurs. Lunchtime tempura on rice was fantastic, they said. I knew they were right because they bought me some. They weren't to blame; no one could dislike them.

Proceed to Joey Kanazawa. He was tense, staring at his screens. Couldn't blame Joey Kanazawa. He tried to invite me in.

Caleb Zucman was last. The first trader I saw. How could he think I'd fit in? No markets, consumers, or traders around. No fights, no wins. For the first time, I wondered if he wasn't the first trader I'd seen. Maybe he never traded.

I looked back at my screens and realized I had taken my phone out of my pocket and was browsing. Nobody there, mate. You've rejected family, friends, and girlfriends. Always text Wizard—she understands.

No text to her. I put my phone away and waited. If you wait long enough, another trade will arrive. Maybe that's when I went crazy.

***

Senior management assigned me a young Japanese guy named Kousuke Tamura as my junior trader, bringing the number of men on my team doing one man's task to four, like a set of fucking trading Russian dolls. I guess someone realized I wasn't right. Kousuke spent all day every day constructing a massive trading spreadsheet to analyze all STIRT markets as he had no work.

In the afternoon, Kousuke selected the entire spreadsheet, deleted it, and started over. In the next day's quiet time without Hisa, I asked Kousuke, "Hey listen, did you delete your whole spreadsheet yesterday?"

Kousuke nodded without hesitation, his visage an Easter Island monument of sincerity. I was confused.

"What the fuck? What the hell, guy! Why!?!?"

Kousuke gazed over both shoulders and then at me intently.

Do not finish work. Never finish work. Finishing work means more work."

For me, this was problematic. Because I hadn't worked in a year. I traded little in my last nine months in London. I got most of it from Titzy. No trading was needed now.

No, I wasn't lazy. Somehow I lost capacity. My work capacity was gone. I quit giving shit. Fuck, I couldn't purchase a sofa. If not for my heart starting to burn after three hours without food, I would have stopped eating. Showering every day was becoming difficult.

I still made money. I always made money. That was simple. Just bet on disaster. Death of the economy World end. That was my last link to mankind. I lost even that suddenly.

I used to work at 8 a.m. Although there was fuck all to do, everyone arrived around eight. All market activity occurs during London and New York trading hours, which are Tokyo afternoon and night. At 8 a.m. in Tokyo, only fish are awake. Still, we had to enter.

Just a little trading was left. Little yen FX swap company. It may have taken 20 minutes, but if I went all out, it could take 10 a.m. After that, what? Nothing. I talked about the economy with Arthur and Kousuke and practiced Japanese with lunch connoisseurs. Actually, they were as busy as I was, but they were amazing at appearing to work.

I wasn't. I slept after 10. With my feet on the desk, I napped. Feet on the floor, I napped. Wake up with a burning stomach and hurry to purchase noodles. I checked Ritzy's progress with the London desk's PnL sheet after he took my former job. I took my 300 one-yen coins in a bag to the cafeteria floor to buy odd Japanese delicacies and green tea. Nothing existed. Nothing. To do.

He hated it. Hisa loathed everything.

Japanese culture has a strange habit of not expressing anger. They often cause themselves physical discomfort.

I'll demonstrate. In a textbook for beginners' Japanese, iie means no. The dictionary says this is the right word, yet nobody uses it. Why? Nobody ever declines! A wobbling nasal grunt is an internationally approved sound indicating "no," but you may only use it with pals. With distant friends, you never say no.

What do you do if someone invites you to get out on Saturday and you have a hot date? Do you decline? Of course not. As if suffering from toothache, you tilt your head to the side, grimace, and sharply inhale through your teeth. Your abrupt discomfort tells the other person no, so they back off.

This became Hisa's habit. Problem: I didn't comprehend. If I put my feet up on the table, Hisa would hiss like I'd stepped on his foot. I would look at him confusedly and try to fall asleep. Hisa contorted and breathed throatily and slowly, like the fucking Japanese Saint Sebastian, removing an arrow from his back. I'd raise one eye and worry him. Hisa would boost his game till he appeared like he was having organ failure, unable to express his anger. My mind was progressively going crazy. I started taking frequent pauses from the desk to brush my teeth and use the bathroom. But men can only brush their teeth so often.

I got down and pretended to work because there was nothing else to do, possibly what everyone behind all those skyscraper windows is still doing now.

Not good for me. The heart hurt more. I lost weight I didn't have and had to see a private doctor for more PPIs.

I cooked to distract myself. I cooked a lot in London, but in Japan I always got everything wrong—beef was pork, pig was beef. Why does Japanese beef look like pork?

Being unable to cook, I would prowl Akasaka's dark alleyways at night like a ghost hunting for food. There are several nice restaurants in Akasaka, yet none speak English or have an English menu. I would enter a sushi restaurant and shrug, but they would sit me down and feed me. It was costly yet never filled me up. While floating home, I'd buy a Big Mac.

My inability to sleep at work affected my home sleep. A cold sweat woke me up at 2 or 3 a.m. When that happened, I put on my trainers and ran to the Outer Garden and around the Emperor's Palace. About 5K to run around. After that, I might sleep for an hour. If the gym on my building's top floor was open, I'd run 5K on the treadmill. I ran a

5K in over 18 minutes. I tried to beat 18 minutes one morning but had to puke up in my room. After my gums started bleeding, I went back to the doctor, who advised me to cease brushing so hard.

***

People began to worry about me. Now I weigh 55 kg. Caleb and management worried. They may not have noticed how tiny I had grown, but my work ethic was embarrassing. Caleb promised the bosses a youngster bringing 100 burgers to lunch. He had a child who usually slept or brushed his teeth.

He invited me to his gorgeous Yoyogi residence, near Meiji Jingu and Yoyogi Koen, Tokyo's largest shrine and park. I met Caleb's wonderful children and wife, who had dealt with his lost thermostat. All of them were wonderful. Dinner and drinks were shared.

But something crucial was lacking. Nobody saw me withering away. Nobody saw my absence.

I searched for something meaningful in Caleb that night. I reached out to him, searching for anything human and tangible to cling onto. Nothing was there. He left.

6

More attempts were made to cheer me up. Especially Florent LeBoeuf. Florent LeBoeuf was in my LSE year and knew we were old pals. The boy was new to me.

Flower was chunky and gamey, with bad posture, like a dirty teddy bear. He traveled to Japan to sleep with as many women as possible (a frequent goal for gaijin in Tokyo), but he was paranoid that Japanese prostitutes were trying to take his sperm. I liked the poetic balance between his dreams and anxieties.

Florent knew exactly what to do to cheer me up. I went to Roppongi with the young gaijin traders he called.

Tokyo has various nightlife districts, including Roppongi south of Akasaka. Under a massive elevated expressway, hustlers sell ladies and kebabs. At the end of the road, a giant orange Eiffel Tower towers above it all.

Gaijin is Roppongi's specialty. Gaijin visits Roppongi. As I recall, most Japanese felt uncomfortable speaking English and would avoid Westerners when I lived in Tokyo, and many still do. Assuming one percent of Tokyo's thirty-eight million residents are young ladies with a fetishistic passion for foreigners, that would be three thousand, eight hundred women. All those women are in Roppongi.

Starting in a little tavern fashioned inside like a train cabin was odd. The clientele was classic Roppongi: foreign-looking bankers (like myself) and dangerous-looking Japanese women.

We each drank one can of grapefruit drink at a convenience store on the way there (Strong), and Florent ordered another. I learned from Florent while we waited.

"See those two girls over there? You can obtain them. One of them. One or both. Which do you prefer? You decide. Anyway, Go there. Say hi. You grin and bow slightly. Make eye contact. Introduce yourself. Give your name. Ask to buy them drinks. Get them drinks. Pick one. Talk to her more. Touch her arm. Ask her to join you at that corner. You take her home. Bam!"

I didn't request this course, but I liked its pointillistic approach. At Gas Panic nightclub, one of the merchants approached a female he had never seen before and started making love with her without saying a word, as if to undercut Florent's carefully planned strategy.

I felt queasy. Maybe my face showed it. Florent wrapped his huge arm around me.

No worries, mate—you don't need to. Come on, guy. Going to a strip club."

***

"Do you think we should do something?"

Now that Kousuke had been brought over to be my junior, a decision had been made to recall Arthur back to Sydney, sadly separating him from his girlfriend. It was his second last day on the desk. He was eating sushi from a clear plastic box.

"About what?" He spoke full-mouthed, loudly.

"I dunno…you know…About the economy."

"We already did something, we bought the green Eurodollars."

"You bought the green Eurodollars, I already had them. There's no point buying more at these levels. Besides, that's not what I'm talking about."

"What are you talking about then?"

The last of the rice was being shoveled in with chopsticks.

"I'm talking, you know, economics!" Do you think we should do something about economics?

Arthur had finished his sushi, so he snapped his wooden chopsticks in half and dumped them into the plastic container, then sealed it shut.

"I don't know what you mean."

I was getting a kind of a stabbing sensation in my left temple.

"Arthur. I'm talking about the economy. Should we do something? About the economy. What the fuck is there to not understand?"

Arthur chewed that for a bit and he moved his chair closer to mine, and then leaned in as if we were about to do a drug deal.

"So…We're not talking about the green Eurodollars here…Am I right?"

"For FUCK'S sake Arthur, this is not about fucking green Eurodollars! The economy is going to be fucking shit for fucking ever! Do you think we should do something about that!?"

Arthur withdrew his chair about a meter and he balanced me, with his eyes. For a moment, he tried to smile. The smile hesitated and pondered a little. Arthur leaned into the desk with his arms.

"You're fucking serious, aren't you?"

"Yes, Arthur, I am fucking serious, do you think we should fucking do something about the fucking economy!? Fucking hell…"

Arthur paused so he could reload an extra-loud laugh.

"What are you gonna do mate? You gonna become fucking Prime Minister? You gonna save the whole fucking world??"

"Well I don't fucking know, what the fuck do you think we should do? Sit here and do fucking nothing?"

"Ahhhh mate. Things are all right mate. We didn't do anything, we bought green Eurodollars! And we made a ton of money. You don't need to worry mate, you're gonna be fucking minted. You've got this whole thing figured out!"

"Yeah, but…" Yeah, but fucking nothing. It passed through me. I knew he was right. "I dunno…I just…I don't know mate. It just…? It doesn't feel right."

"You're being ridiculous mate. What the fuck are you talking about? What could you even fucking do anyway?"

"I dunno. I could go back to, back to university…Maybe? Try to show the guys there that they're wrong."

I thought about the universities, about the dusty pointers locked up inside them, inverting matrices in little rooms with no windows, and the idea of them changing the world. Then it was my turn to laugh.

Arthur went back home after that. I'm pretty sure he's still a trader, not yet the leader of the free world. He'll do it though, I reckon, eventually, after ten or fifteen million pounds.

7

Arthur left and winter followed. It was frigid and treeless. Tokyo winters are different from London's. The sky is blue and sunny all day. Kousuke was my only companion without Arthur. Kousuke was a polite, honest, hardworking boy. He was like Japanese teen anime protagonists—unexceptional yet determined. No matter how many times he finished the spreadsheet, I knew he'd never quit.

I wanted to know him. He didn't seem crazy, which was rare at the time. The issue was his limited English. My Japanese improved, so we spoke more. He informed me he had memorized five new English words every day for fifteen years. This surprised me because his English was terrible, so I requested him to show me his words for that day. First on the list was "notwithstanding." Then I noticed his English was fine, only with an accent.

Once this issue was resolved, our communication improved rapidly. I learned his staccato-Katakana English and tried to speak it. This improved my communication with Kousuke and Japan.

Now, Japanese people say they don't comprehend English, yet they do in Katakana. Katakana, a Japanese phonetic alphabet, makes English words sound Japanese instead of "black pepper" or "table." Ask for a "a-i-ro-n," and it will be in your room. Ask for an "iron," and they'll be confused.

Knowing how to talk to Kousuke was a comfort. After not talking to non-crazy people, you realize how much you need it. I invited Kousuke to dinner.

Kousuke introduced me to okonomiyaki on Tokyo's East Side, the shitamachi, where he grew up. Okonomiyaki is a savory Japanese pancake. I guess cabbage dominates. It's huge, tasty, and approximately fiver. The London price is £25.

We pulled off the roadway and climbed a narrow wooden staircase. A sliding wooden door, silver bells, and a booming, greeting "irashai!" Inside, bow through cloth.

Inside was all wood and warm lighting, with antique Japanese movie posters from the 1950s on every wall. Large pancakes steamed on metal hot plates were served at low tables.

Kousuke was quiet and independent at work. As we sat down, he screamed loudly. A cat-like waitress appeared abruptly. "Toriaezu—biiru." The beer comes first.

I had plenty to say. I informed Kousuke that my girlfriend back home was coming to Japan but was not yet there. I was confident I hadn't hidden this, but no man in the Tokyo office was afraid to sprinkle exotic women on me. Kousuke sipped his beer and mused.

I told him I hated Hisa's incessant twisting, grimacing, and watching. Kousuke grasped this. Everyone saw Hisa as "a man with a very small heart."

I went on to tell him that Caleb had once been my mentor and idol, that I wanted to restore our relationship, but he was gone.

That one may have been lost in translation, but Kousuke expressed his sympathies. I felt I should go on since those sympathies were so genuine.

I requested this dinner to notify someone, possibly anyone, that I was quitting. I will leave this time. My plan was to wait until January for the bonus, then tell Caleb I was done. That I would labor for charity and keep all my deferred stock. That Caleb had done the same before and would let me.

Many Japanese are hard to read. Not showing emotions on their faces. But Kousuke stared at me and tried to speak. He looked worried about me.

***

I had my bike. From London it was flown. I usually spend the weekend on it.

I'd bike south to the orange Tokyo Tower. Family Mart is a first-floor convenience store next to my doctor's office, nine meters taller than the Eiffel Tower. Buy a milk carton there. In the park below it is Zojo-ji, an old temple. Sometimes I heard Buddhist monks singing, and when the tower turns on at night, the temple shines black before the orange.

I'd bike west to Meiji Jingu's massive torii gates, Takeshita Dori, or Yoyogi Koen's big square, where middle-aged guys with Elvis haircuts dance and fight to death on Sundays.

I'd cycle east to Shiodome, where they took the tops of the mountains and filled in the sea, then to Tsukiji Market, where huge tuna heads pile up in buckets with their cheeks scraped out, and to Hama-rikyu-teien, where an old Japanese lady sells beautiful sweets and green tea for 500 yen.

I would bike north to Ueno Koen, where you can feed turtles and carp, or to Senso-Ji temple, where gray, wizened, bent men and women shake little wooden boxes that reveal their fortunes.

Sometimes I went all the way around to Odaiba, the large false island in Tokyo Bay, which took a long time because you can't cycle across the bridge. I sat on a wooden pole near the false beach and watched the sun set over the city and Rainbow Bridge light up. There's a fake beach with a sea you can't swim in and a fake Statue of Liberty.

I returned to London for Christmas and spent two weeks in a hotel in the Westfield shopping mall in Stratford, the worst location in the world. The Wizard grabbed me, and both my legs started shaking.

8

2013 NOW. RECKONING. I knew the day was coming.

Bonus day was solely remembered for the Frog giving it to me on a giant video screen and Caleb being in the room. The number was written in yen and seemed huge. I recall my PnL but not the number. What must I have obtained after making 18 million dollars before trading and stopping? Eighteen times seven. Six million dollars. Something like that.

After that late January day, the countdown began until the money struck the bank in early February. I checked the account daily. I had to plan to talk to Caleb on Friday after the money landed on Thursday. But I didn't. Say what? Coward, perhaps.

A rough weekend. My mood was shaky. Something shifted under my skin. The Wizard had moved 300 kilometers west of me to East Osaka, near Nara. Not sure why she did that. I told her I quit via Skype. She was happy and always urged me to quit.

Monday. Caleb invited me to his corner office. Caleb demanded a corner office to return to the bank. Because he told me, JB, and Billy that night last summer when we drank by the Thames. I could see miles west and south. One robust wooden table, two sturdy wooden shoulders. Big trees concealed the Emperor's Palace behind them.

Caleb seemed vigilant and serious when I entered the room, which was unusual. I assume he knew what I was about to do, given the timeframe, but I never thought of it. Only the clenched eyes and mouth caught my attention. Mid-motion muscle grabbed and held. Chess, poker, wolf.

I sat. As usual, he looked down and I looked up.

Did he anticipate my remarks?

Of course, I told him.

I rarely plan, thus my speech was unrehearsed. I needed to say I was leaving, sorry, that I would work for charity (something about unfairness), and that in gratitude of all he and Citi had done for me, I would work the remainder of the year for no bonus, but ultimately depart. Really, this time. In 2009, Caleb had offered the Slug the year without a bonus, so that last addition was an artistic flourish.

I missed my beats and fell regularly. I discussed my stomach and heart in extended rants about illness. My trainers (why always the trainers?), Gas Panic, and Quentin Benting were mentioned inappropriately. I may have seemed crazy.

Did Caleb soften as I fell? Did his eyes sparkle when I stated I was sick? Honestly, I don't know. I think I wasn't there. Like my delivery, my speech memory is vague. Not remembering speaking, I'm piecing words together.

When I finished, I remembered how he shifted in his chair. I immediately sensed a tinge of tenderness that was fake. Hold onto compassion. Nothing to grasp in this dude.

Caleb regrets. He was terribly apologetic. He knew I struggled. He relocated to Tokyo as a young guy. He understood how lonely and chilly it may be. However, the bank wanted me to stay. They appreciated my work. Take time. Do not rush. Don't rush. Come back. Talk to me in two weeks.

***

I felt like the cartoon character that jumps from a skyscraper, lands on a trampoline, and bounces back. I returned to the STIRT desk.

I was not—something had changed.

Something started when an hourglass was spun. Despite my brain's ignorance, I knew it in my bones.

Despite not knowing what was wrong, I had a feeling. I quickly requested a meeting with HR via email. I wanted Caleb to be unable to cancel my deferred stock or hinder my exit.

I had to sneak into HR. I kept my mistrust to myself.

***

Icicles modeled chairs in windowless rooms before me. Tall, blonde, Swiss? Maybe Swedish. Her fingers were long and thin. Without a flaw, she shuffled papers and measured my eyes.

Can management cancel deferred stock? Naturally, they cannot. Can you leave the bank and work for charity while keeping your deferred stock? Never heard of that; will investigate. But Gary, you OK? You appear agitated. Tell me you're not fully present. No worries—we'll safeguard you.

That didn't reassure me.

9

With the keen edge of winter wind, the next two weeks reached me. To visit the Wizard, I boarded the train west to Hyotan-yama in Higashi-Osaka. Kyoto Station bullet train exit. Change again at Yamato-Saidaiji.

Near the Wizard's home in Nara is the "Yamayaki," or "burn the mountain," celebration. Since the Wizard was teaching English at a local middle school, I went alone to see it. They burn Mount Wakakusa, turning Nara's historic temples dark in orange.

The whole mountain on fire, fireworks, massive crowds, and smoke are magnificent. Setting a mountain on fire may be risky, but the fire engines were there. They trimmed all dry grass around the mountain to prevent the fire spreading.

What about me? Did I trim all my dry grass? Would fire engines rescue me?

***

Two weeks passed quickly, and I was back at the desk. Time for my second meeting.

It appears Caleb did not hold this meeting at his office. He probably didn't want the Emperor to see. He led me to a windowless white chamber in the building's core.

You have two weeks to think about it. Do you still want to leave?

What could change? What could've changed?

Yes, I am."

"OK. Well… I researched leaving the bank to work for charity. I regret to inform you that bank management must approve the option. Bank management will not approve."

He grinned. Big, shiny piano teeth. I guess the bank owed me almost 1.5 million pounds by then. It may have been two. I was too old to remember numbers, so it was above my "more than a lot."

His message was plain. You can leave, but money stays.

I disliked that. I disliked that. No one robs a bank that way.

The realization in my bones eventually entered my brain.

Then war. They desire conflict.

I told myself, no problem. It's not your first conflict.

***

My life soon became a joke. In what I now call "the Meeting Period," I only attended meetings.

I was suddenly scheduled for three or four meetings daily. Some days were two or five, but meetings supplanted trades as my life's foundation.

All meetings were with top executives, but the mix varied. If I met with Hisa Watanabe in the morning, he'd smile and pat my back. In the early afternoon, Rupert Hobhouse and the Frog would video call me and explain my decline in somber tones. I would stare at my feet and nod. Tonight, Caleb was in the room and the Slug was on the screen: we believe in you! You can!

Between Hisa, Rupert, Caleb, the Frog, the Slug, and the many, many other managers I'd never seen but were suddenly eager to join the fun, the permutations and games we might play were limitless. Rupert and the Frog liked sharing wisdom and talking about themselves. Hisa and the Slug love support and encouragement and are nice. Caleb liked Good Cop/Bad Cop and The Hairdryer unexpectedly.

The Shootings were my favorite meetings. The Shootings were always fun. "We've Been So Good To You!," "How Dare You!", and other shouts were made by Caleb. They were always better in person, when fingers could poke faces. I worked harder to ham up videoconferences, where people could mistakenly leave their microphone on mute, because they lost a lot of impact. Yes, I liked The Shootings since they reminded me of childhood and are rare as an adult. I wondered if they ever worked. Changing one's mind would be odd, right? Just shouting in one's face. I wonder if anyone does.

The meetings emphasized Man Up And Make A Choice. Would I Be a Man and Work? Was I going to Fuck Off and Leave?

Risky choice.

The Imparting Of Wisdoms was perfect for this feeling since you saw how people thought. The Frog sat me down on a video conference from London and informed me that even if I could have kept all the money (which I couldn't), it was never enough. I made how much after taxes? What was it? Two million pounds? He laughed loudly at that figure. That wouldn't survive five years! Again, pleading on my hands and knees! I stared at my shoes while we laughed.

Rupert was fun too. I liked him. He talked a lot about his dad. Former Army Dad. He complained about his bonus to His Dad, who encouraged him to man up. Not sure how that was relevant. I think I should man up too.

The role inconsistency was the best part of all the meetings. Since this was not a Citibank strategy, I shouldn't have capitalized it, but it gave me hope. So colorful! So much drama! So much theater! Never knew who you'd receive! Caleb's Bad Cop act was often followed by the Slug's Good Cop, and he was pleased to attend both sessions on occasion. These events' stark contrast was wonderful. Caleb's rapid transformation from snarling wolf to teddy bear gives you hope for humanity. No one bothered about these contradictions. Chess has no dishonest moves. I seemed to be the only one who noticed them. As for me? Yes, I adored them.

I invented a game to combat these methods. I mastered Try To Say Nothing For As Long As Possible as a toddler. The title explains the goal—only grunts are allowed. This gave me something to play for, but the Frog and Rupert one-on-ones were surprisingly simple to win. You have to do a lot with your eyebrows in Caleb's confrontational meetings.

In none of these sessions did I address the Leave/Stay Dichotomy that was continuously put at my feet. No way. Fuck them. I wouldn't go without my money. Never again will I work for them fucks. I would benefit most from being fired. That way, I could leave and get paid. What the hell were they doing? Nah, no way. Fuck them.

Fuck them. Fuck them. Fuck them. Fuck them.

They may kill me with their yells.

***

My lack of choice, and probably my lack of speaking, led to a Final And Very Big Meeting with all top management present or on the line. Since The Slug was the priority, The Meeting Would Be Very Nice.

The Slug gathered everyone and made his case. He acknowledged my illness. He believed. Thought it was true. The bank would do everything to help me get healthier. Help with medical, practical, or emotional issues. I got what I needed. He only needed my dedication. Be present. To trade. To make money.

He advised relaxation and letting go. Avoid stress. Take Your Time. It's fine, he said. All of us will support you.

After that, he went through each top manager and said they believed in me. Wonderful. Soul-enriching. Heart-warming. Caleb spoke with tears.

I tried a new game afterward. I trusted Slug completely and accepted him at his word. I Took My Time to Be Well and Take Care of Myself. My contracted hours began.

Contractually, I worked 9–5. Japan may have nine-to-five contracted hours for everyone.

No one works 9-5.

With senior management's consistent support, I took a calm and holistic approach to my work. Every day, I took an hour for lunch. Sometimes an hour and a half! I walked to the Outer Garden in Tokyo's cold air to count trees. I considered Leaning Into It when I was sleepy. I slept with my hood up.

Wonderful. Very soothing. I made the most PnL in Tokyo in one week. Last week of my career.

The next week, after 9 a.m. on Monday, Caleb softly stroked my shoulder and asked me if I wanted to go to dinner with him the next night.

Naturally, it happened then.

10

THEN, ON A large, affluent, fat-fingered man with a loathing for ill-positioned thermostats painted a vision of my life for me on a chilly, dark Tuesday evening in February 2013 in the nameless sixth-floor ramen restaurant of an unknown Marunouchi shopping complex.

Courtrooms and destitution were the future, years of bank theft wasted.

One of the world's largest firms was behind its brutality.

You think? When you're twenty-six years old, one of the world's most profitable traders for one of the world's biggest banks, having come from nothing and fucking £12 a week paper rounds, and your idol sits across a table from you, over two bowls of ramen, and looks in your eyes and says, "Sometimes bad things happen to good people," what do you think? We can complicate your life."

Like a thug. As if a don.

You think?

Nearly ten years had passed before I was expelled from school. I wasn't a drug dealer, but the kids at my grammar school, which was elite, knew I could acquire drugs.

I could acquire drugs. They were right. It was true. I got narcotics from my street's dealers. There are several. Drug dealers were on my street but not theirs. Because rich kids asked me to procure them drugs, I got expelled.

I and other kids have more options than those drug traffickers. They cannot attend LSE. Investment banking internships are not won by card games. They sell drugs because they have no other way out of poverty. Sometimes they commit fraud or burglaries. Some make money, some don't. Some go to prison, some don't. Kids like that occasionally have terrible luck. Sometimes stabbed. Sometimes they die. Sometimes people wait in cars outside nightclubs for them to cross the road and run them over, causing their bodies to spasm on the floor. That instant, I understood we're alike. Everyone's the same. Drug traffickers, bankers, traders, Caleb, Saravan, Brathap, Rupert Hobhouse, Jamie, Ibran, JB, me today, me then. Everyone's the same. Our dads' wealth was the only difference. They would be on the trading floor with me, Arthur, and JB if those drug traffickers went to Eton, St. Paul's, or whatever Rupert's fucking boarding school was. Buying green Eurodollars. If those merchants were born where I was, in Barking Hospital, East London, where Bobby Moore, John Terry, and a million other tiny hustlers sold penny sweets on school holidays, they'd be selling drugs on the corners too. We're identical. Everyone's the same. Stupid. Smart. Young. Ambitious. Wishing to be. Not sure. Chasing something without knowing what. Running to and from it.

For young, hungry hustlers, selling drugs or fucking bonds is the road. Everyone's the same. Nothing distinguishes us. Sometimes God shakes the wrong box, in the wrong temple, and someone like me or Billy falls out backward and lands on our faces in the wrong game, on the wrong board.

We're identical. You don't beat us. You don't beat us. Start to finish, two different games. From the start. Since birth.

Now you don't think much. Dreams overwhelm you with that stuff. You focus on the plump face and think, "Mate." If you're not a gangster, don't talk like one."

I knew I would fight immediately.

No decision was made. Sometimes you have to face the devil.

Was it smart? Was fighting Citibank wise? Among the largest corporations?

I dunno. Fuckit. I never claimed wisdom.

I slept no sleep that night. I vomited at home. No fuckfood. Bile is weak and piss-colored. Due to tablets, no acid. Wipe your mouth and pace. You pace and pace.

Fucked it. Really fucked it. I had no strategy. What the hell can you do now?

Already contacted HR. What he said was true. I couldn't work for charity without their approval.

No way was I leaving without the money.

But it wasn't the game anymore. Much more was to play. The entire situation changed. It was my turn to defend.

Will they sue me now? For what?

Nothing on me could have been his. By hand, he would have shown it. To clarify, I was fucked.

But did he need help? He probably didn't. Like in 2009 when politicians declared they would tax banks and everyone scoffed. They knew who was boss. They could likely do the same to courts. Talking about Citibank. They likely sue anyone.

Still, though. Walking isn't enough. They need something. Was there anything? Would anything exist? Had they any power over me?

Grateful for Billy. Cover, thanks. Your. Arse. I covered mine for a while. I was clean. I knew. Nothing existed. I played clean. From the start.

Haven't I?

Was there anything? There might have been. I made how many trades? Hell, it must have been millions. Chat conversations: how many? Broker calls: how many? Every single one recorded. Documented, filed. Every single one was there. All of them. What did I have? I had nothing.

They could always paint with that evidence. FUCK.

You do what?

Maybe they overplayed. Perhaps they assumed I was bigger than I was. Maybe that's why management never questioned how I made so much. Maybe they suspected a shady plot and didn't want blood on their hands. Perhaps they thought it was the only way shady guys like me could make money, either by selling drugs or doing other crap. Maybe they do that. Maybe their lives are like that. Fucking and pooping up their grease-covered poles.

No. No. Gary. Unproductive. You need a fucking plan.

OK. Finished. Must move first. You must move immediately.

When does the doctor's office open? One near Tokyo Tower. Google it. Nine am. OK. You phone that fucking office at 9 a.m. to obtain the first appointment. You claim insanity. Ham it up. Talk about not eating, sleeping, or losing weight. That's not exaggerating, but add something on top, anything. The most important thing is that you receive a sick note before leaving the medical office and sending it to Caleb, HR, and the Slug ASAP. Try it. You've increased the bar for them once you accomplish that. A fabricated case against someone who just applied for stress-related sick leave is different. It'll look like a request for punishment. Safety is assured. A disability law? Do you know disability law? Nothing. Don't get furious at me—what else do you have?

Nothing. Not a thing. We had a plan and will follow it.

Should we seek advice? Now what time? Two am. In London, everyone will be awake at 5 p.m. Who can advise you? Billy? Snoop? The shit is mine. I'll fucking fight my stuff. I'll fight and win.

Only Kousuke was texted at 2:30 a.m.

"Kousuke, something strange happened. Never tell anyone I text you. May I meet you immediately?

I texted my bosses at 5 a.m. to say I couldn't come in because I'd been throwing up all night. There were three hours to kill. I ran around the palace at night.

I sped around the palace, winter air on my fingers and face. Dinner memories kept coming back. Caleb wanted to shake my hand at the conclusion, but I had no idea if I did.

That implies I fucked up.

***

5 a.m. Send text. No response. Good.

Lots of time between 5 and 9 a.m. Can you sleep? Set an alarm. Unable to sleep. Run again. Last time you ate?

Nine am. Phone the doctors. This doctor is for foreigners, and the receptionist speaks English. The first appointment is when? 10:30.

Tokyo Tower, 20. Big and orange under blue skies. Take a seat, receptionist. Doctor's office, 10:30. Punctual. Settle down and look crazy. You already seem insane. Can you look madder?

Tell him all.

My boss is threatening to kill me."

No. Too much, wind it down.

"My boss is threatening to sue me. Very afraid. I shed plenty of weight."

Tall Japanese man with bald head and white coat. He stares at you with his left eye, as if it's his only decent one.

Two weeks of anxiety-freedom. Sick leave for one month. Written in lovely blue ballpoint pen on a small white slip of paper. That'll do.

Back home. Send email. Doctor worried about you, wrote you anti-anxiety medications and one month of sick leave. Tell them you need the rest of the week off because you're a disaster. Turn off your fucking Blackberry.

Gary, sleep. Get to sleep.

***

Woke up in the middle of the night. I don't remember what time it was, but my room was black even though I fell asleep with my clothes on and the curtains open.

I didn't activate my BlackBerry. Fuck that. I no longer needed that crap. But I checked my phone. I received a text from Kousuke about eleven.

"What happened? What's wrong? I can meet tonight or tomorrow."

He sent it midday. Tonight was probably hopeless. I requested a meeting the next day.

Outside the okonomiyaki shop, I met Kousuke. God knows my appearance. From his expression at me, Kousuke probably looked like a fucking disaster.

I may have been shaking as I told Kousuke what happened over beers. Kousuke's mouth gaped. He was shocked. Caleb is freaking nice. He really is! You would like him if met. I swear. Everybody does. Everyone did.

Kousuke said nothing after I finished. Sitting with his mouth open, he caught flies.

He understood it was his turn to speak.

That's illegaru!

He shouted three times.

I know it's illegal, Kousuke. No one cares, mate. The world's biggest fucking bank is Citibank. They can do whatever."

"No! They cannot! It's Japan! Rules apply! Breaking laws is prohibited."

"Kousuke, I think not breaking laws is a pretty fucking international rule mate, and that hasn't stopped them, has it?

Kousuke was enraged. He carried it in a hidden way in his and my country.

You must record it. It must be recorded. Buy a recorder. Make him repeat."

He visited Yodobashi Camera and arrived at my building on a blue bicycle late the next evening. He handed me a little portable voice recorder and instructed me to record everything. Make him repeat."

Well, what about Kousuke?

Good child.

***

Next few days, what did I do? I drowned. Back to work on Monday.

I was properly removed from the yen book. It was returned to Hisa. Touché. I merely entered the workplace to stroll into a meeting with Caleb.

This meeting would be intriguing because I was introducing a new strategy. Make Caleb As Angry As Possible To Record His Mental Statement. Strangely, I was excited. It would change style drastically. Over the weekend, I practiced utilizing the portable recorder. It was a four-inch cylinder with a red record button. Since I couldn't push the record in the middle of the meeting, I walked to the bathroom and hit the button before putting it in my pocket. I had tried that at home, but I was always afraid I would touch the button again with my thigh and turn it off.

Entry into the trading floor and office. Time for a game.

Caleb was calm from the start. He lost his storytelling flair. Such a shame. Very different from the restaurant patron. I needed old Caleb. Keep going! Prick him. Nothing. Like drawing blood from a stone. Fuck! Why hadn't I considered this before the restaurant dinner? Why didn't I videotape it then?

Maybe he knows. Perhaps your unexpected expansion has drawn his attention to your pocket bulge.

No matter, keep going. Hell, what's to lose?

"We regret this outcome. We regret your decision."

"No apology! You cared nothing about me! You never let me try! You had Hisa fucking stuck in my rear from the start! How can I trade with him behind me? Timing my restroom breaks! The hell were you thinking of keeping him? Everyone knows he should have been sacked!"

Oh, Come On! Now he shouts. Cracking up. We got him! " It was you who never tried. You haven't been serious since arriving. You always intended to leave! Showing up the day after bonus day to quit. Since you arrived, it was your plan! Did you not even consider it? You went straight to HR from my office. Do you realize how I appear with you in Tokyo doing nothing? I moved heaven and earth for you! What does this make me look like? After my service to you? I hired you! I made you! You were nothing! That money we gave you!"

I should have let him run, but I didn't.

"Do I owe you money? Listen. Citibank made ten dollars for every fucking dollar I made. You know it. You know the truth. Without me, you would never have succeeded."

That silenced and sat him down, and I smiled with joy. I realized the whole point was to get him fucking talking, so we sat silently for a minute.

"So. Am I getting sick leave?

He returned to the meeting's Caleb. Cold, professional, detached. I fucked it.

"Your sick leave cannot be approved. The company doctor decides."

11

Strangely, I was back at the STIRT desk. Between Hisa and Kousuke, with no work. I studied kanji in Japanese textbooks.

I was furious that the meeting yielded nothing. I shitted about the company doctor. Caleb's words showed he had HR covered. Having the company doctor was mandatory. I'd be fucked if the company doctor rejected sick leave. Staying at the desk would kill me.

Hold on. Please wait. Maybe we have something. He said what? "You went straight to HR from my office." That's not allowed—should he be working with HR? You shouldn't tell him you went to HR after your first meeting about leaving. He shouldn't know, right? Shouldn't that information be private? Fuck, maybe you have something.

Send HR an email requesting a corporate doctor meeting.

Dear Icicle,

Please meet to discuss my sick leave application.

Warm regards,

Gary Stevenson

Friends, return to the windowless room. Remember to record this time.

She remains chilly and indifferent. Impossibly straight stance. Such tremendous straightness made me feel like a rat.

Nobody cared—no one looked. There's a plan this time.

"Can I ask you?"

My first move.

"Yes, Gary, what's the question?"

Were our meetings confidential?

She wasn't expecting that. Did she sway? She could have done it in a blink.

It depends."

It depends? You mean it depends?

It depends."

How about fucking what?

She placed both flawless hands on a pristine Moleskine notebook back. You shouldn't swear to HR.

"Not all conversations are confidential. Gary, it depends."

OK, so," I was getting frustrated. "What's confidential?"

"Well, if you suggested hurting yourself, I'd have to escalate that."

I'm not talking about injuring myself. Did you tell Caleb when I asked you about me leaving and working for charity in early February?

"No, I didn't."

She replied quickly. Way too fast.

Are you sure?

"I did not tell Caleb about that meeting."

Brief pause. Going to do this? We'll do it.

"OK, so why have I just left a meeting with Caleb, who told me you did?"

A significantly longer pause. I know how long it was because I've listened to the recording multiple times. The time was 47 seconds. A one-on-one meeting has a considerable pause.

Icicle was still during the interval. Still as a statue. She never touched the notebook's back with her long, slender fingers. No mouth tremors. She kept her eyes still. Was she thinking? She probably didn't blink.

My vibrations were gentle. I observed her and wondered if her hair swayed in the breeze.

Finally, she stated: "I investigated your deferred compensation and leaving for charity work. Nothing can stop you from doing it. Beyond the bank's control."

Well. You say what about that? Still fighting in the rat.

***

My next stop was the company doctor. Three levels down, he was distant from the trading floor. A middle-aged, salt-and-pepper-haired, cheerful Japanese man reclined low on a plastic chair with his arms on his big stomach in a small, brilliantly lit workplace. Young, attractive Japanese nurse in uniform stood behind him.

Man sat me down. I was asked what was wrong. It seems he cared.

Well. I suppose I should explain. I cried after speaking for a minute. I could only cry to them. I'd never met them.

I don't think I recognized how messed I was until then. Sometimes I convinced myself it was just a tactic or game. Maybe it wasn't a game. Maybe it was my life.

I received three months paid sick leave.

***

After that, I hesitated. Wavering, I didn't move.

I was at the atrium edge again. I peered down but didn't jump.

Now I had my sick note. I didn't request leave.

I went back to the trading floor to get my string bag after leaving the doctor's office, then returned home.

Somehow, the matter got out of hand and beyond senior management that day. I know because the London lads started texting me.

Don't quit, Snoopy texted. You can win! You're brighter than those jerks!"

Titzy texted, "It will be a shame to see you go man, I thought you were going to run this place one day."

Billy didn't text me till late at night. It said, "All right Gal? Management stated you're leaving and keeps pushing me to keep you. They said you requested stress-related sick leave. Up Gal? R u OK?"

I simply responded to that message.

Stop worrying about me, boss. I'm always fine."

Probably a lie.

***

So. Why didn't I request sick leave?

I warned myself it was risky. I worried that applying for sick leave would cause bank legal action.

Was that real? Was that risk real? Are you protected against lawsuits for using sick leave?

Looking back, it was probably more. I probably understood it. No more PnL, Liquidator. Young men with ambition no longer envy.

I met with Rupert because the meetings kept going. Rupert and I were alone in this encounter. He appeared on the video call in Caleb's bright skyroom.

I sat and examined my shoes.

Gary, no one believes you. Nobody believes you're sick. They assume this is a gimmick to gain more money or get out of the bank with your delayed stock so you can work for Goldman Sachs.

Staring and nodding, I did nothing. I sometimes did long mental divisions.

"But I trust you."

That attracted my interest. I looked up at the television.

Gary, where do you want to be now? If you could go anywhere?

After some thinking, I answered him honestly.

"Nowhere. Never want to be anywhere. Actually Hobbs, I don't care."

"How's Harry?"

"How's Harry? He is fine. Yes, he's fine."

Rupert didn't know we'd split or that I hadn't spoken to Harry in nearly a year.

"Imagine playing football with Harry on your Ilford street. Is that your preferred location?

Harry was what age when we started playing football? He was maybe five or six. I must have been nine or ten then. How old was he when he outperformed me? "Yes. Yes, I suppose. Yes, I would."

These street days were long gone, and the lamp post, telegraph pole, and recycling center concave wall were far away. We often kicked the ball into the recycling center and had to clamber round the side. Over the massive iron bridge, over an old man's garden who shouted at you from his window, and into the recycling center with its twenty-foot-tall stacks of soiled newspapers. After kicking the ball over, you'd climb back around and play football again. In winter, we played until someone's mom shouted supper time. Sometimes my mom, sometimes Harry's mom. Sometimes we ate together, sometimes alone.

"You can get there. You can return there."

No way, I'll never talk to that kid again.

It's OK. Everything will be OK. So keep tough and get through this. You will be fine." Why was he doing this? Rupert did this, why?

"Thanks Hobbs. I appreciate it. Thank you."

That's OK, you'll be fine."

Signals off.

I sat alone in the office, watching the Emperor's Palace. A personal phone text arrived. It was Rupert.

Apply for sick leave. The bank is helpless. They have nothing on you."

So I did.

12

Three months.

Three months is short. It felt like forever.

I hadn't had three months off since I was 19. I spent much of it fluffing pillows.

It felt like breathing.

I took the bullet train to Hyotanyama initially. Change in Kyoto. Change at Yamato-saidaiji.

The Wizard lived in a little plastic apartment her school gave her. Your nose almost touched the roof while you slept on a ladder shelf. Many young Japanese live like that, with no kitchen and frosted windows.

Since the only warmth was a little air conditioner, winter was usually frigid. We owned it, so we didn't share.

She was astonished but not surprised that I went there without telling her.

We would climb the ladder and throw the futon to the floor, where I spent a lot of time. She would heat a cup of ramen and ask me if I had watched good movies.

We dressed warmly and went to a Hyotanyama park despite the cold. She laid down a picnic blanket on her front, I inched my head into her little back, and we read books. Or we'd visit Nara's large parks and see the old wooden temples. Feed deer.

Even on sick leave, meetings continued, but on my phone. I set the phone on the speakerphone on the futon and lay on the floor next to it. I spread myself out like a starfish and looked up, over my head, through the frosted window, upside down, as managers chatted. I saw the distorted blue sky slowly turn black.

Wizard would often sit next to me and grab the phone, then hang up and say, "Come on Gary, that's enough of that."

***

I flew home to visit my mom. I don't know why we were never close. I drove her from central London to Regent's Park on my small black Vespa, acquired with my first bonus. We strolled around the lake and gardens. I asked her why she never played guitar.

Strangely, she looked at me. My peers looked at me strangely then. She asked me, "Gary, are you OK?"

I replied, "Yes, yes. Yeah, I'm OK. I'm always fine."

***

On the journey home, I saw Cool Hand Luke for the first time with the world's most attractive man, Paul Newman. He's messed up, so he's sent to prison and joins a chain gang.

The bully gang leader challenges Paul Newman to a fight. Paul is smaller and can't fight, so the bully keeps hitting him. He gets up a thousand times until he's battered black and blue. Bullies eventually surrender.

Paul Newman—what a dude. Wonderfully gorgeous man.

***

My sleeping and eating were strange while I floated. I slept during the day and scavenged for food at night.

No place was better, I swear.

Tokyo provides lots of food for the lonely man, and spring brings warmth.

A small ramen shop was near my building. They made chicken and pork ramen. Clear, fine, vinegary broth. Tasted great. It's closed now. I generally slept through that place's short opening hours, but then there came Yoshinoya. Dear Yoshinoya, my nighttime queen, your dazzling orange windows never disappoint. Daily beef on rice in Yoshinoya. Always tasty, fast, and inexpensive. No limit on pickled pink ginger. Sometimes they sell eel.

Green peas were unavailable in Japan. Sometimes I miss them terribly. They ultimately appeared in Saizeriya, the world's most Japanese Italian restaurant chain. Cheap, substantial amounts, appreciated by students, they mixed green peas with bacon and served with a barely cooked egg.

Not all meals were fast. Sometimes I was up early enough to enjoy steak frites at Toranomon's French restaurant. Citibank kept paying me.

In Tokyo, you can feast like a king without money. Free sushi would have sufficed. Sushi Zanmai, Kamiyacho, three times a week. Rice with marinated tuna, tsukedon. Big size (oomori) same pricing. For 500 yen, it includes miso soup and green tea. I got a 100-yen discount certificate every time, so it was 400 yen. £2.50! I chatted with the sushi man at the counter.

Be kind to yourself. Enter an Izakaya. Request umeboshi ochadzuke. No need to thank me. Have fun.

Freshness Burger. In order, miso/shio/shoyu/tonkotsu ramen. Kanda has the best karashibi ramen. Takadanobaba back alley banh mi. Cold soba with 7-Eleven brown sauce. 7-Eleven tuna mayonnaise onigiri. Famichikin. Gyoza from Azabujuban. Every day, tuna on rice for breakfast (if you've just woken up). Fu-u-u-u-unji noodles dip. Yayoiken-grilled mackerel.

All these venues were open and full of lonely males. That was especially true of ramen joints and Yoshinoya late at night. Lonely males eat wonderful cuisine in a line. They brush shoulders and elbows while dipping chopsticks in bowls. After paying 600 yen, they leave.

What better place to be depressed?

I woke up fully clothed in the middle of the day and checked my phone. 12:37 p.m. Harry missed 127 calls.

I thought while sitting in bed. His birthday was the day before.

13

I suppose I should move immediately. One should not await retribution.

Yes, yes. Had enough ramen. It was time for legal representation.

Messaged Sagar Malde. Remember him? The LSE Kenyan guy. He worked at Lehman for two months before the 2008 crash and knew those who sued. I requested him to put me in touch with someone who knew about that.

I hired three lawyers—one in the UK, one in America, and one in Japan. It was pricey, but Citibank had raised my income to £120,000 a year when they sent me to Japan, so the attorneys, sushi, and ramen were on them. I suppose I should be grateful.

The lawyers didn't tell me anything I didn't previously know.

Can a bank sue you for doing nothing?

Of course, they shouldn't legally. You wouldn't be the first.

Can I work for charity and keep deferred stock?

The paperwork says yes. How does paperwork hurt Citibank?

Should I sue the bank?

You could, but you'd be in court for years and owe two million pounds.

Ah, court forever. Your thoughts on court forever? Didn't we want to avoid that?

But what are your options? Not much to do but wait. You rest for three months and sleep during the day. Get some weight back. You return after three months, apply for charity (you must locate one), and hope it works.

The plan wasn't foolproof.

I found a wealth inequality video online. Wealth disparity was rarely discussed then. An LSE anthropology professor from South Africa wrote it. I informed him I wanted to work for a wealth inequality organization via email. He connected me with one and we met. They promised to assist me flee.

That was my only job. Waiting for my time to end.

With the attorneys, philanthropy, and weight on my bones, I felt more confident. I had a strategy and game. The thumping in my gut and heart persisted. I probably felt fear. I experienced a dull thigh ache.

I often lay on the floor. Belly down near the window in the sun. It was exactly what I did as a kid when I was expelled and had no school. Lying on the floor by the window, completing arithmetic homework on a wooden board.

I was afraid to return, which doesn't make me proud. I feared running out of three months and having to return to the bank.

Soon, three months passed. My first meeting was with the company doctor. I admitted my fear when I entered. My fear of returning. He nodded and wrote to me another three months after looking in my eyes.

***

Late May is a lovely time to visit Tokyo. The start of the rainy season makes many Japanese dislike it. The city heats up quickly and the sun shines brightly. When you go outside, the air is so humid it feels like a hot towel on your shoulders.

Liked it. I enjoyed it greatly.

Japanese call "rainy season" "tsuyu," and its Chinese characters, "梅雨," mean "plum rain." I had never witnessed hot plum rain in England. Heavy, hot rain falls in thick walls like sea waves.

If I was caught in a rainstorm riding my bike, I'd be saturated in 10 seconds. I had a whole pair of clothes in a plastic bag in my rucksack and had to change when I arrived. I loved it when it rained hard with a strong wind, hot rain in your face.

When I got writing that second three months, I thought, "Could it be this, then, forever?"

Could I keep living this way season after season, sick? I would never work again if I was sick forever. The seasons would pass, and I'd cycle through rain my whole life.

How about that? Would that be good? Is that game good? A good life? I cycled more at night when it wasn't too hot. My favorite cycling spots were Shinjuku and Shibuya. These two neon palaces would blur your eyes in the rain. Shinjuku's Kabukicho was one of my cycling trips. Tiny bars with intoxicated Japanese people were ideal for practicing Japanese.

Near the Prince Hotel and away from the bars, I parked my bike near the south end. I wanted to go through neon-lit alleys with other lonely males.

This big plaza facing the hotel has rails where I locked my bike. Taxis line a huge road in front. Sitting in three lines, they purr. Yamanote line green trains cross a bridge to the side. Tall structures and enormous neon signs everywhere. I can see the skyscraper district on my right, west of the road, one black tower covered in white metal cobwebs. Yoshinoya, orange-glowing across the street, adds meat to rice. A massive LED screen the size of five houses rolls and shines over it. Kyary-Pamyu Pamyu dances on screen with a huge crimson bow.

A scorching wind slapped my face as another train passed.

I suppose I should settle here.

***

After that, I tried harder. Study Japanese, make friends.

Had a nice middle-aged Japanese tutor. Her name was Yoko Ueno. She wore a mask in every season: summer for humidity, autumn for cold and flu, winter for dryness, and spring for pollen.

I discovered "English Language Conversation Cafés," where insane Tokyoers speak foreign languages. Chatting with nutcases while drinking tea. It fit me then.

My favorite English Language Conversation Café was in Takadanobaba, a student neighborhood north of Shinjuku. I like watching students. Summertime groups would go blind drunk and fall through the streets, then someone would collapse to the floor. That would require their pals to pull them up, but they would lie there and shout, "I'm OK!" The goal was to stay on the floor as long as possible. Friends usually raise you. Unless they do, you sleep there all night.

I was improving. I thought I was improving. However, I had missed five months of work.

As I spent more time away from the office, returning seemed unattainable. When I told Wizard about my sick leave, I sometimes felt overwhelmed. Very minor twinges in the corner of my left eye and arm shaking began.

Wizard placed her hand on me when that happened. She never mentioned the shaking, but she did say, "Why do you fight them Gary?" No need to fight. You've had enough. Why don't you leave?

She was wrong. Never enough. I'd never leave. Leaving them win would be wrong.

14

My second three months of sick leave were almost over, and I was confident it would be extended again. I was healthy and sick.

Kyle Zimmerman emailed me a week before my doctor appointment. Kyle Zimmerman, the Icicle's employer, was an American and Tokyo HR head. He was little and rat-like. That resembled me at that time. I thought that was fairer.

He detailed a legal technicality about my debt in his email. It had a lot of documentation, but the summary was straightforward.

Over six months of work means losing all pay.

Perhaps not a sabbatical, but I doubt anyone cared.

Inside, I spoke to the doctor. He made it clear: no returning. I told him it wasn't my call. I was forced to leave.

Speaking to me, he put his hand on my shoulder, which is unique to Japanese. After staring at me, he spoke.

"I suppose it can't be helped."

***

The Wizard visited Tokyo. I told her I had to return.

She saw my fear and her pain.

"Don't go," she said. "Avoid it."

We both saw it in her green eyes. No sleep, more weight loss.

Not that Wizard—it's not a possibility. I must do it."

"You choose to do it! No need to do this! You're done! You can leave anytime! Why are you hurting yourself?

It doesn't matter. It doesn't matter how I treat myself. I must do this."

She seemed tearful at me. She pursed her lips and didn't cry or say what she was about to say. I may always wonder what she would say.

We broke up later that day. I returned to work a week later.

***

Strange things happened the day before I returned to work. I was eating at my building's rooftop restaurant. The Prudential Tower was no longer my home. I had moved to Atago, which has a modest shrine on a hill up steep stairs. A samurai once rode his horse up the steps to give plum flowers. It took 45 minutes to descend.

No longer on the thirtieth floor in my new building. The ninth story was still high, but my new flat faced up a hill above a graveyard, so I could see tree tops from my window. Really enjoyed that.

My upscale corporate apartment complex has a top-floor private restaurant. I would eat there often if I was awake during its opening hours because the pricing was surprisingly low.

I always ordered a salmon, avocado, rice bowl with an umeboshi, the world's sourest and tastiest circle dish. A Japanese waitress in her late 20s or early 30s felt it was humorous that my face would curve up every time I ate it.

After dinner at the restaurant, I found a small, handwritten letter beneath my door the day before I returned to work. The message simply stated that you appeared melancholy in the restaurant. I hope all is ok. Contact me at this address if you need to talk. Maki.

I returned to work the next day.

15

After six months on sick leave, no one phoned me. Slug and Caleb didn't call me. No more management meetings.

I was officially HR. HR super-rat Kyle Zimmerman. Apparently I had removed the icicle from the board, a skillful move.

Billy taught me early on that "Talking to HR is never a good thing." I botched that one.

Kyle Zimmerman had a corner office in the small HR department. I walked through the department to get there and tried to make eye contact with the Icicle, but she never looked up.

The windowed office was tiny and organized. One wall was lined with filing cabinets. There was little decoration on the desk. One notepad, one pricey pen. Kyle grinned and had life in his eyes as I entered.

Of course, I was filming everything, and I pondered shouting and throwing accusations to get an admission or slip, like I did with Caleb. I listened because I was curious about their ideas. I couldn't be reinstated on STIRT?

Smoothly animated Kyle spoke. Elan and efficiency. He was relieved I was well. Very funny, almost laughed. He was glad they found me a new job. That was hilarious too. Kyle Zimmerman's dark approach was appealing; I wish he'd attended more meetings.

Kyle walked me to the trading floor. I admit, my heart skipped a beat. Everyone, especially Caleb's ponderous body in the far corner, was visible.

I saw the STIRT desk in front of me, but we didn't go. Kyle guided me right, then again. Turn around, past the printers, into a nook. I met Gerald Gunt there.

Gerald Gunt was the most dull person I've met, on or off a trading floor. His soul seemed to want death, and his glasses were more alive than his eyes.

I realized I wasn't at my best, but now... Me against him? Blood returned to my fingers. I figured, I can win this game.

At the time, I had been without wins for a while, so the concept seemed encouraging. I grabbed his hand strongly.

Hello Gerald, I'm Gary."

***

My promotion to "Business Management" was decided. I didn't know what business management was then and still don't. I just know Gerald's department. A spreadsheet was made. Paperwork was done.

No smile from Gerald. Gerald never smiles. But he looked down and put his spectacles up his nose. He carefully got up from his chair, using his last willpower. He walked to the world's saddest workplace, and I followed.

A sickly blue halogen bulb buzzed and sputtered on the wall as Gerald Gunt's office's only illumination. Broken ceiling light. Wasn't everyone?

Gerald Gunt has a monotonous, lengthy voice. His voice was so dull it bordered on intensity. The mournfulness was profound, like an echo, like a lost whale's moans.

He explained my job. I didn't listen. I scanned the room. This must be the place where you wait to go to hell but there's an administrative delay. It was plain save for one personal touch. Probably Gerald's wife's framed photo was on the desk.

The photo showed his young wife. Perhaps in her mid-20s. She was lovely and Japanese. The girl smiled. He grinned too. In the photo, he must have been the same age. God, how old is he? No way to tell. Gerald, what happened? Gerald, what happened? Where did you go? Was your turn wrong?

My time in that office looking at that photo must have been long, since Gerald was finished. I smiled passionately and sought to crush his hand.

***

I learned nothing from Gerald's speech regarding my job. I recorded the whole incident, but I never listened to it again for fear of aging myself.

Gerald's email describing my duties after our meeting was a relief administratively.

Long, tedious, meticulous spreadsheet work made sense since Gerald was a spreadsheet man. The amount of work he assigned me was huge from my brief email scan. It would take weeks or months.

The end. After my trepidation of returning, this was all they had. This was all they had. Putting me in the corner by the recycling bins and making me type Excel lines like a permanent fucking jail. I was paid $120k a year for that. Well, screw it. Despite many detentions, I've always been a dick.

Started a fresh Excel sheet and finished in 15 minutes.

Gerald invited me into his office two weeks later to check my spreadsheet. Looking forward to this.

I emailed him before the meeting.

He was confused when he opened it.

What's this? Where's it? Is this all you did?

I grinned at his boring gray eyes.

Yes Gerald, that's all I've done."

Nothing here! No work here!"

Scratched my hair and frowned my brow. That was worrisome.

I apologize, Gerald. Is there a problem? I know you asked me to do that!"

Gerald was defeated after another smile. Meek will inherit earth.

***

Gerald never assigned me any work after that. Nobody did.

Never once did anyone speak to me. I had nothing to do. Kousuke would sneak by and leave an onigiri on my desk occasionally when he was sure no one was looking. The trading floor and bathroom were connected by a long corridor, and sometimes Caleb would come toward me from the opposite direction while I brushed my teeth. He would always pretend to have forgotten his passcard and turn back.

After understanding the situation, I emailed Kyle to ask him how many holiday days I had.

Throughout my trading career, I took a few vacations. Naturally, the prior six months had been sick leave with no holidays. I took six weeks off after he informed me I had over fifty days.

***

Autumn came, and I traveled. Since Wizard and I had gone to Kyoto numerous times, I opted to visit Hiroshima, where okonomiyaki has noodles.

It was surprising how straightforward the bank return was. I thought the police or attorneys would have taken me to jail. I didn't expect a well-paid job with no work and easy printer access. It meant what?

Did they really have nothing on me? Had they searched without success?

Attending the Takadanobaba English Language Conversation Café numerous times, I spoke to many people. I often chatted to Japanese folks, but the café also attracted international outcasts. I had tea with a middle-aged Dutchman with sandy brown hair and a huge nose for several hours. He married a Japanese girl when he was young and divorced her. He became a priest and stayed.

My whole narrative flowed as I spoke. No one knew the complete story or that I was a millionaire. As the Dutch priest nodded and drank beer, I probably talked for almost an hour. He said, "Fock man," when I finished and waited. That's messed up."

***

I took my sister back to Hiroshima and to the holy island of Miyajima, also known as Itsukshima, where the huge, red torii gate is in the sea.

I stripped down and swam through the gate, and we fed the deer at night.

My sister asked how work was doing, so I showed her my office desk drawings. One John Lennon, one Paul McCartney.

My sister didn't understand my work scenario, so she squinted at the photographs and then at me and asked if I was OK. I laughed and answered, "Yeah Debz, I'm always OK."

She laughed because she knew it was true.

***

In late autumn and early winter, I studied Japanese, kanji, and Beatles drawings full-time after returning to work.

My drawing improved. A junior staff member, who likely didn't know about my extended confinement, passed my desk and saw my work.

"Hey! That's great! Is it Ringo Starr?"

"Thank you. Yes, it is."

That's great! You're great! Its purpose?

"I'm unsure, quite honestly... Possibly something like... Development of creativity? I want it to appear like this photo."

I showed him the source photo. He appeared bewildered.

"Yes...but... What's the purpose? How do we use it?

I said nothing. That question confused me too, and we shared a momentary, intimate bewilderment. He nodded and backed away after a time.

***

After several weeks, I realized that I had a lot of free time due to having no actual work, so we unanimously agreed to reduce my working hours to one or two hours a day after a meeting with all of the office's people who were talking to me, which was no one.

I started studying or painting at ten. Sometimes my lawyers gave me documentation to print on neighboring printers. At twelve, I'd get lunch and go home. Kikanbou Karashibi Ramen in Kanda was my favorite lunch spot, where white-shirted salarymen sweated tremendously while eating outrageously spicy ramen in a small,

138

smokey, darkly lighted room with red demon masks. Spicy ramen would tire me out and prepare me for a good nap.

I continued for weeks. I went to the talk café in the evenings and met this Japanese waiter at the Beatles Bar in Roppongi on weekends. She was cute, spoke no English, and helped my Japanese improve. She would sit on the floor in my large corporate apartment instead of the sofa. One day, she turned and asked, "Hey, how do you afford this place when you hardly ever work?"

I wondered if I had discovered the best job.

16

In December 2013, Kyle called me into his office. I wanted to be fired, which would have been amazing.

Kyle smiled while sitting me down. Great rat smile.

He inquired about work.

Yes, it's great. I do great stuff. How're you?

Yes, it's good. This is good." His smile ended. Why not apply for charity?

"The charity route?"

The charity path. The Icicle said you wanted to apply."

"Oh! The charitable route! This is true. I want to apply."

"That's nice, so why not apply?"

"You know... I have a load of work...

"What kind of work, Gary, are you doing?"

"I doubt Kyle would grasp it… It's quite inventive."

Smiled again, he turned to his computer. I received leave documents from him.

***

That development thrilled me, as expected. I had to walk through the door.

Did I want out?

I see now that my situation was unhealthy. I lived in fear of being sued and was not free. Since I was smart, I had to yield when senior management glared at me.

Though it hurt, my quality of life was good. I was getting my first Japanese girlfriend, my Japanese was improving, I had a lot of half-friends from the conversation café, and I had an amazing list of restaurants. Also, Christmas was coming. I gave it time.

***

The Japanese are bad at Christmas; they mix Santa with KFC. Chat cafe crazies celebrated with karaoke.

I still disliked karaoke. I'm not a poor singer, but I was self-conscious. After I sang my song, Hiroshi, a proud white-haired sixties Japanese man, sat me down.

"In karaoke, good or bad singing doesn't matter. What is important is that your guests enjoy themselves."

Karaoke became more enjoyable after that. Maybe that's a life lesson too.

***

I paid my respects to Hanazono Jinja on New Year's Eve at midnight with a café group.

In Japan, New Year's Eve temple visits at midnight draw long lines in the cold and dark. Some wear traditional clothes.

Tokyo's biggest red-light district, Kabukicho, houses Hanazono Jinja's historic shrine. Shinjuku Golden Gai has little pubs for professional drunks, alcohol, sex, and wonderful food everywhere.

I learned Japanese at those bars, especially my favorite, the dilapidated but welcome "Kangaroo Court Decision." I always ordered grapefruit-flavored shochu there. I'd progressively add more shochu to my cocktails until they ran out of grapefruit and the proprietor had to run to 7-Eleven to buy more.

My half-friends from the café and I waited a long time at Hanazono Jinja. Most Japanese spend New Year's Eve with their families, thus we were all freezing, familyless folks at the Jinja.

To the front. I tossed a golden five-yen coin into a wooden box, which bounced until it fit. Metal/wood. I shook the hefty rope, and the bell rang tinny and clanged. Twice I bowed, clapped, and waited. The frigid air returned to my lungs suddenly. Midnight air is cold and damp. It didn't burn me this time.

I suppose it's time to go home."

***

It took me until late January to gather my documents. To be honest, I took my time. That charity hired me. They allowed me to write about inequity from London for an American nonprofit. Though Japan made it easy to forget, the global economy had continued its slow-motion decline, with little growth and declining living standards. Sometimes I worried if they kept my prior trades or locked them out. I assumed they didn't keep them, but they should have. For whatever reason, leaving for charity required a huge paperwork packet. I applied after wading through.

I received an email response a month later.

"Your application was denied."

That may have affected you like it did me.

Why did they ask me to apply?

The answer was apparent, thus the question is foolish. They proved I was trapped.

They showed me that I could eat all the gyoza in Tokyo if I wanted. I could ride about the city for months, party with Beatles lovers, ring New Year's Eve bells, and swim through historical shrines. I could do everything if I wanted. But I couldn't leave. Unable to return home.

How long would it take to withdraw all the money? Three more years? My age would be thirty. Screw that. Fuck him. Fuck them. What was the point of the game?

I pushed the red button on my always-with-me recorder, put it back in my pocket, and stormed down to Kyle uninvited.

"What the fuck are you doing!"

Kyle was thrilled. It nearly made me happy.

"Gary! So glad to see you! Are we meeting? Please sit."

Sat down.

"What the fuck are you doing?"

Gary, what do you mean? This is about what?

"You know what this is about! What the hell are you doing?"

I'm sorry Gary, but I don't understand. I doubt this meeting was planned. Is something wrong? What happened?

"Why did you reject the charity application?"

"Oh, the charity application!" Leaning into his chair, he smiled. "Now you've done that. What's wrong?

What made you reject it?

"Well, let me see."

I couldn't see his computer screen, but he looked. He hummed a gay song I didn't recognize. I wondered if it was Japanese.

"OK, I understand. The charity you applied for is not US-registered. The criteria are not met. You cannot work for them. I apologize."

He smiled again as we watched. Great rat smile.

"I know your fucking doing."

Sorry, I don't understand."

"You, the Icicle, and Caleb lied to me. The Icicle illegally discussed secret discussions with Caleb. What do you think?"

I'm sorry, Gary, I don't know anything. What are you talking about?

You fucking know what I'm talking about! You've been cooperating from the start, and you know it. What do you think?

That was impossible. He was uncatchable. Get him mad, draw him out. He fucking liked it. He loved shit like a pig.

"I'm sorry Gary, but I don't understand."

His smile was lovely. I swear he nearly winked.

***

Nothing to do. After returning to my desk, I emailed Citibank HR the official definition of a fucking charity. Three weeks passed without a reply. I dumped the Japanese girl that weekend. No more fucking girls seeing me cry while my life turned to ashes and bone. I ran around the palace again. Remove all fat, fucking fat. Remove all unnecessary fat. Remove everything unnecessary.

What if I couldn't leave? What would I do? Would I sue the fucking bank? Would I sit on the trade floor for three more years like the fucking ghost of Christmas Past? What would I become? What would I become? Would I quit? Turn back? Become Caleb? As Gerald Gunt aged, would I gray?

My sleep was ruined quickly, and I became a night creature again. In the late winter, the nights were still cold, and I rode my bike around the town with icy breath hunting for food.

Police stole the bike around then.

No one steals in Japan. Nobody steals fucking stuff. You can throw your wallet on the ground and retrieve it three days later without losing any money. But police will steal your bike, so fucking watch it. Avoid station front parking.

I asked my building receptionist how to get my bicycle back from the police. I went to the address given. I took the damned train.

I arrived at what was likely the world's largest bicycle impound. I've never seen that many bikes in one location. A bicycle universe. Nobody has stolen more bikes than the Tokyo police. I suppose they must use their time.

I was taken to my bike. They found it precisely thanks to contemporary engineering. It took 15 minutes to walk there.

The wheel broke. Not sure how. It was a dumb custom size, so correcting it was difficult. It would have to be created from scratch. I had the bike longer than I had a girlfriend. It was the only thing I flew from London. That was my closest connection to an old pal.

My bike was left outside the station. The station where I fucked up. Tokyo cops, steal it again. I then visited an old, second-hand bike store in a quiet residential area behind Yoyogi Park, near Caleb's former house. I asked a creaking, old, bent-over man in Japanese to show me the shop's cheapest bike.

He took me to a tiny, funny yellow "mama-chair" with a basket and bell. I tried to ring the bell. It was somewhat broken. All of us. He told me it cost five thousand yen, around £30 at the time. I gave him money and rode home. Sometimes you lose old friends.

***

The spring of 2014. Cherry blossom and slowest email war.

Citibank explained its charitable definition in three weeks. I was almost positive my charity met this criterion. I had to gather all the documents to clarify this and email it to Kyle Zimmerman. It took him a month to respond. It seems out I signed page thirty-six of that second application in the wrong location.

It was obvious what they were doing and could last. I wondered if they would keep paying me to sit in Gunt's corner forever. Then the blossoms fell.

My mental health declined dramatically. After the Icicle told me there was no stopping me from going, I felt like I had an escape route. Indeed, I had never known how strong a rope it was, but I had always known it was there. That confidence gave me a chance to breathe away from the wolves for the first time in a while. I was back on the trade floor, and I couldn't leave.

I spent more time at the office despite having little to do. I ran at leisure because I couldn't enjoy my former activities. Rainy season returned after the cherry blossoms faded.

Citibank then acted. They terminated my housing.

***

Citi had paid for my house in Japan. As is typical for banking expats in Japan, a large housing allowance and my still-high salary were supposed to entice me to move.

My apartment's balcony overlooking the graveyard and the restaurant with umeboshi were nice. I could see Tokyo Tower if I bent over and craned my head from the balcony, and that restaurant on the forty-second story was wonderful for people-watching. A Japanese man and his wife once listened to an American banker discuss Moby-Dick for an hour without speaking. All they did was hum and nod. The banker grinned and waved at me as he left, but the Japanese man had his head in his hands over his shoulder.

144

Since the restaurant was vacant in the evenings, I would sometimes watch the fireworks over Tokyo Bay from the dark restaurant in summer.

No more pyrotechnics for me, I suppose. The rent was high, and if the bank didn't pay it and I left the industry, I could barely afford two months. It was obvious that I was fucked and wouldn't work again for years. I budgeted as if I would never be strong and healthy enough to work again, probably forever.

My friend, from Romford, Essex, near where I grew up, relocated to Japan to become a Power Rangers stuntman. It was his childhood dream. He rented a poor room in a shabby apartment in Shin-Okubo, in Korea, the closest thing central Tokyo has to a ghetto, near our English-language café, where he worked. Asking to sleep on his floor via SMS. He replied, "Yes, man. No problem."

I wondered whether Citibank would keep pounding me with silly random crap until I gave up and walked. I figured, let them hit me. Not giving up. They won't start.

17

After that, it was hot and damp, and I went crazy again.

I was tired of waiting, so I tried something new.

I started emailing lots of people, different folks every day. I repeatedly emailed the CEO and Global HR Head. My lawyers neither advised nor authorized these techniques. They were my creative touch.

I forget what I stated in these emails. I sometimes called them by fashionable and unique nicknames or talked about obscure topics. I sometimes made particular references to Caleb, the Icicle, and Kyle Zimmerman. I sometimes hinted darkly that those things would look bad in newspapers. Other times, I would share funny stories or chat about cuisine. I sprinkled Mormon scripture throughout the Global Head of HR's correspondence after learning he was a Mormon. I liked that touch.

After two weeks, Kyle Zimmerman called me into his office at the height of summer.

I knew Kyle Zimmerman would welcome me. He always was.

I knew Kyle's office well by now, and he had a family portrait on his desk. Kyle's wife, like Gerald's, was Japanese, and so were his three children, who were probably half Japanese. I bowed at the waist and stared at this portrait for a long time as I entered the workplace. Only then did I look at Kyle. His appearance changed. His smile was constant. Not with his mouth, but his eyes.

A whole inversion was wrong. Upside-down Kyle Zimmerman.

I was enthralled, so I sat down before him and spent some time looking. Then we had a long talk that altered everything.

In stories and life, things happen we can't talk about. You and I have experienced them.

This can happen for several reasons. Perhaps we cannot breach the trust or memory of a lover or close friend. Perhaps we cannot name or speak our deep emotions.

Sometimes we can't speak because of our heads. This is why we don't inform our mothers when we make £400,000.

Other times, the reasons are external. Society sometimes writes our names on paper, twists it into a ball, and puts it in our mouths.

Which one happened to me? Did any?

The answer is unknown. Honestly, I'm sorry. When we cut ropes that bind us, we may cut our skin. Kyle's smile after that meeting will always be remembered. Real happy, not pretend happy. He was truly joyful. After shaking my hand, he seemed proud like a father of his son.

I thought, Fuck you, rat. You and I are fucking rats.

Finally, I was free.

18

I WON HOW? How did I win the fight?

The reason is I was crazy. Because I was smart and daring. I was original, imaginative, wild. That I broke free from my artificial restrictions and went insane.

I don't know. It probably wasn't.

The Slug was fired a week before I was released, exactly when I was writing ridiculous emails to C-level management. Not sure why. I'd like to think I was one of the reasons, but I doubt it.

Several sources tell me that after Slug was fired, he arranged a video call with Citibank Global Sales and Trading and thanked everyone for their work beneath him, then broke down in tears. Right on the line. Before everyone. Every senior manager in that conversation, who disliked the man, wiped a cold, melancholy tear from his eye.

I don't know who earned my freedom because of the Slug's shooting and my spiral into lunacy. Was it me? Or the Slug?

The Slug had always been kind in my meetings, so I assumed that Caleb, not the Slug, had been keeping me at the bank, paying me a £120,000 annual salary, plus housing, to publicly humiliate me and prevent me from completing the escape that had slipped from his hands.

Maybe I was mistaken. It was maybe never Caleb. Perhaps it was all a ruse. Maybe the Slug kept me there, and Caleb let me go after he departed.

Not sure. Will never know. How I won the game is unknown.

It's like that, right? You never know how much luck and skill are involved, right? That Russian linesman, who wasn't Russian, may have prevented England from winning the 1966 World Cup. Avram Grant may be the best manager in the world if John Terry, who was born where I was, doesn't slip in the Champions League Final in Moscow. If Ilford County High School had called the police on me in October 2002, I might have had a criminal record and been one of those boys with no options, peddling drugs on street corners forever, and none of this would have happened. You never know? How much luck and skill?

Perhaps I outwitted Citibank. My game may have been excellent. Maybe I didn't do that. Maybe I just kept rising up, like attractive Paul Newman, and getting punched in the face. How can we tell which wins and losses were luck and which were skill?

Trading is similar, right? In 2011, and 2012, I made money betting on the collapse of the global economy, the slow but certain collapse of living standards for ordinary people and families, and the descent of hundreds of millions of families across the world into inescapable poverty, which did happen, but did I win?

Yes, I bet on those things almost every year from my sofa and bedroom until 2023, and yes, more and more families fall into ever-worsening poverty and can't pay their mortgages or feed their children. But is it skill or luck?

We don't know? Maybe we'll never know. How do we proceed? Let it happen or stop it? Should we close our eyes and say it's a game? Tell ourselves it's luck?

Rich economists, with their small hearts, nice suits, and even smarter accents, are also sure in their accuracy. They believe, like me, that things will improve and that our issues are temporary. They've been wrong every year since 2008, and they and their class keep getting richer, but isn't that just luck?

No way to know, ever? Who is right and wrong, what to do, and whether to change. We must wait and see, right?

Arthur may have been right about there being nothing we can do. He didn't say you couldn't do anything, right? Some action is possible. You can too. We can wager. Betting the end of the world. Be sure interest rates will be lower than inflation and the economy will collapse. That home, stock, and gold prices will rise, enriching the rich as wages stagnate and collapse. We can, right? Everyone can do that. Can we all get rich if we do that? Can't we? If we're lucky. Everyone can profit from the end of the world, but we can only watch it crumble.

You know, I had a childhood pal. His mother was his lone parent, and his family was poorer than mine. His mother often skipped meals so the kids could eat, thinking my friend and his sisters didn't notice. But they noticed. I know. Because he said,

I suppose games are like that. Winning and losing are possible. What's more important than winning? No idea. Nothing comes to mind.

19

I requested two weeks from Kyle.

Why I requested two weeks is beyond me. Perhaps I wasn't ready. I didn't know I'd be freed that day. I needed time to inhale.

In those two weeks, I worked every day for full hours. Yes, my nine-to-five contract hours.

Why did I do that? Not sure. Perhaps I wanted to hear the sounds. No, that Tokyo trading floor wasn't mine. The trading floor did not make me famous. Not the trade floor in my dreams.

Still, it was a trading floor. Men competed to make money, be right, be better, buy flats without doors but with spinning walls, and have all their ambitions destroyed. Young youngsters can appear from nowhere and become the best in the world, but rarely do. Old and young rich men notice them and think, "Look at him, with his stupid Topman shirt." What does he have that I don't?

As we've mentioned, maybe they're correct and it was just luck.

I still hope it was lucky sometimes. God knows the future is bad if it wasn't.

***

My last trading day arrived. I said a few goodbyes. I saw Florent Leboeuf and laughed over his recent womanizing. He promised to contact me next time he was in London. He never did.

I went to lunch lovers and told them about our meals. They exclaimed, "Oh Gary, your Japanese is so good."

Last, I spoke to Kousuke and thanked him for everything. He grinned and waved his hand in front of his nose and muttered, "That's OK, that's OK," in Japanese, and I never saw him again.

I left the trade floor without applause, but I looked back once.

20

I went and unlocked my yellow bike. It was tethered to a bankside lamp pole. After putting my luggage down, I unbuttoned my striped white shirt, scrunched it up, and put it in. It was very hot outside, so I put on a little gray 7-Eleven vest that Wizard had given me when she first arrived in Japan and always made the staff laugh, and I decided to walk through the Outer Garden of the Palace one more time instead of cycling home.

It was a long walk home, and the sun burned my skin. I walked my yellow bicycle through the million identical trees, trying to count them but getting distracted.

I wondered why I was leaving and who was right and wrong.

Was the Frog right about my money running out? That I would crawl back?

Was Arthur right—there's nothing to do when the world collapses? That we can only profit and watch?

Was I right? The economy would keep falling? Life would only get worse?

And the rest of us? Was anyone right? Was Chuck right to hoard coins and get lost? Was Caleb right? Leave and return. What about JB, Harry, and Snoopy? We were doing what? Was anyone right?

I couldn't count the trees because there were too many. I felt the light on my neck and shoulders and considered taking off my shirt.

However, I decided to leave it since you never know when you'll return.

So the Japanese sun burned my shoulders, I tried to stop thinking, I walked to the sound of cicadas, and I attempted to taste the wet air temperature.

I flew to London to find a losing game.

I decided I don't care if I win, but I should quit playing alone.

Play this with me.
Good luck.

Printed in Dunstable, United Kingdom

63763915R00087